The Innovative Agent

*The Insurance Agent's Roadmap
for Success*

Mark Sisson

THE INNOVATIVE AGENT
The Insurance Agent's Roadmap for Success

ISBN   978-1-61961-401-7   *Paperback*
        978-1-61961-402-4   *Ebook*

In loving memory of my dear brother Amos.

"Mark Sisson's explanation of the challenges facing insurance agencies is spot on, and his guidance on how to keep your agency ahead of the disruption is helpful and tactical. Advice given in this book is not only immediately useful, but it is based upon research, statistics and real-world agency experience. Look to this book for the tools you need to navigate today's ever-changing, technology-driven insurance world."

— ERICA KIEFER, VP MARKETING & SALES, AGENCYBLOC, INC.

"The principles outlined in The Innovative Agent provide insight on how to leverage technology to bring new products to market that customers actually want using the "lean thinking" method. Whether you're a newly licensed insurance agent or an industry veteran, this book will save you time in your next product development."

— MICHAEL BASIAGA, MANAGING PARTNER OF

NATIONAL ONLINE INSURANCE SCHOOL

"Finally, someone has written a book to take insurance agents to the next level. This easy-to-understand book gives you great insight with real life examples to improving your business.

There is never enough time to improve our skills, knowledge and systems that are crucial to our business. Agents have been putting off learning new technology and this is your opportunity to learn and make this a very profitable year by utilizing five key principles that Mark talks about in the amazing book.

This book will shift your focus to the important points often overlooked by the majority of agents selling in this day and age. This is a must-read for anyone that is looking to improve their insurance business."

— PATRICIA A. BERRY, UIRMEDIA.COM

CONTENTS

THE INNOVATIVE AGENT

By Martin Carr

Eighteen years ago, I was interviewing for a job as an editorial assistant at the Health Insurance Underwriter magazine. The woman who would become my boss told me, "You'll like it— this is a really interesting time in health insurance!"

Has it ever NOT been an interesting time in this industry?

In this excellent book you're about to read, Mark Sisson does a great job explaining many of the outside forces that disrupt the way benefits professionals do their job. And there are a lot. From federal legislation to state regulations, and mergers and acquisitions to giant carriers slashing commissions or dropping entire books of business, agents and brokers always have to be on their toes.

You know an industry is over-regulated when its regulations

spawn their own industries (COBRA, HIPAA and PPACA compliance, just to name a few).

The point is: It's not easy being a health insurance agent or broker. It hasn't been for a while, and it's only getting more difficult. A lot of people feel like the world is against them. Only agents and brokers are correct.

I don't mean to depress you. The upside to all this disruption and interference is that only the strong will survive. The cream will rise to the top. Gone are the days of the mediocre agent. It's time for the Innovative Agent.

Every day I read articles written by people in this industry. Most of them contain one valuable nugget of insight or an occasional viable tip. This book contains a ton of actionable ideas that will help you sell more and work smarter. Mark has done a great job of analyzing market forces and laying out a roadmap that will help everyone in our industry.

I wish we could clone Mark, but that's probably some sort of HIPAA violation. In the mean time, enjoy this book. Take its lessons with you and try them out. Be the Innovative Agent your clients need.

— MARTIN CARR, VICE PRESIDENT OF COMMUNICATIONS
NATIONAL ASSOCIATION OF HEALTH UNDERWRITERS

For decades, building a successful career in the insurance industry resulted in exceptional income for those willing to take on the start-up risks and costs. Once established, providing the right products and service made longevity almost a given. Why?

- The need and affordability of insurance provided for a strong and continual base of prospects.

- If you took good care of your clients, word-of-mouth coupled with a good marketing plan ensured you would earn a growing portion of your local insurance market.

- Government regulations and compliance posed little interference in running an insurance business.

○ The environment was static. Open your office for business and the clients would come. Some insurance products were a necessity, such as life and health insurance. Others such as home and automobile insurance, though a necessity, provided for a large prospect base because they were state-mandated insurances.

Disruption from Every Direction

Insurance agents have witnessed breathtaking disruption within the scope of insurance sales, government regulation and technology, particularly within the last five years. The change has been so drastic that without a new business vision and strategy, an insurance business might not survive over the long haul. In fact, as I will explain further, disruption is happening on a faster basis as time moves on, catching unsuspecting insurance agents and agencies flat footed and out of business before they know what hit them. The old management style of "planning, forecasting and hanging out a shingle and they'll come strategy" just doesn't work anymore.

New Technologies

Many sales and marketing tools, such as flyers/mailers, radio ads, billboards and cold calling are becoming less effective or outright obsolete. Newer technologies are coming onto the scene faster than ever before. The insurance industry has seen this first hand. For example:

○ Few prospects "let their fingers do the walking" in the Yellow Pages anymore. Instead they search for insurance agents and products on the Internet. If you don't have an effective website, you aren't considered to be a legitimate business. Being the "local agent" rarely carries much weight anymore.

○ People are gathering and sharing their life experiences on social media platforms, including shopping. If your business doesn't have a social media presence, you are missing sales opportunities.

○ There are many new quoting and direct enrollment platforms available that simplify sales for the consumer. Failing to put these to use can put you at a huge disadvantage. Certain platforms are far superior than others—you just have to find them.

○ Thanks to the advances in cloud-based computing, prospects can easily shop and purchase insurance with their smart phones.

Disruptive Innovation

The most serious threat to your business comes from disrupters. Their strategy is quite simple: they enjoy **disruptive innovation** by using a combination of new and less costly technologies to take to your customers. The speed with which they can disrupt a market can be incredible—greatly destabilizing or destroying mature businesses in months or just a few years.

Disruptive Innovation: *An innovation that creates a new market and value network and eventually disrupts an exist-*

ing market and value network, displacing established market leaders and alliances. The term was defined and phenomenon analyzed by Clayton M. Christensen beginning in 1995.[1]

For the unsuspecting insurance agent, the disruptor just showed up out of the blue. To the disruptor, this isn't just a one-time home run; disrupters don't settle for "one and done." Their vision and business model is different than the average insurance agent. They hypothesize, build, test and implement new products and strategies in alignment with their vision repeatedly, with increasing speed. Just when some of the competition thinks they have copied the disruptor, it's too late. The disruptor has already optimized and begun implementation of a newly improved product.

Insurance Companies

Because of newer technologies and low-cost cloud-based computing systems, insurance companies and the government (healthcare.gov) are creating costly disruptions to the agent community by selling direct to the consumer. If you aren't experiencing competition from insurance companies or from the government in the insurance industry you work in, consider yourself lucky. But don't be complacent. Continued advances in technology may open the door for insurance companies in your industry to begin competing against you.

One of my roles in the insurance business is that of a General Agent (commonly called a GA). As a GA, my agency earns income by marketing insurance company products and value-added services to agents. When the agent writes business, the insurance company sends us an override. So, our strategy focuses on recruiting agents by providing unique products and services that encourages them to work with us instead of a competing GA.

Over the past several years, I have had the opportunity to interview a lot of insurance agents, including those in Life & Health, Property & Casualty and Financial Services. The purpose of the interviews was to find what business problems the agents were experiencing and then find a value-added resolution.

Oftentimes, after asking the insurance agents how we could help them to become more successful, they didn't know where to start. There was too much regulation, lower commissions, less business walking in the door, they couldn't keep up with their website and social media programs, there were continual changes in technologies - mostly problems of disruption.

As a GA, we had a dilemma. We had to ask ourselves: What could we offer to the insurance agent community that would help them navigate around the obstacles of disruption and loss of market share? Time and time again, the answer always came back to having the right business model. The old business model of planning, forecasting and "hanging a shingle" waiting for the customers to show was no longer viable. Instead, agents need a simplified business model that uses innovation, sometimes disruptive to insurance markets, to connect the product with the customer. The product is not the insurance that is sold, but rather the value proposition that makes prospects say, "I want to buy from you!"

Within these pages, you will find strategies to:

- ♀ Create a new business model that thrives in the current era of radical technological transformation, which we will continue to face as time marches on.

- ♀ Build a strong, sustainable business in alignment with your vision while keeping disrupters at bay.

- ♀ Understand the basics of building and testing out new products quickly and with a small budget.

- ♀ Scale your new products and leave your competition behind.

- ♀ Explore how inexpensive "off the shelf technologies" can be integral parts of your product development and scaling, while minimizing internal costs.

This book is not written to teach you about the intricacies of innovation, disruptive innovation or entrepreneurship. To get a more thorough understanding of the content of this book, I recommend you read *The Lean Start*-up by Eric Ries, from which some of the concepts I mention in this book are based. I also recommend *Big Bang Disruption*, by Larry Downes and Paul Nunes, for a much deeper understanding of how disrupters are changing the world we live in.

Though this book is written for the insurance industry, it can be easily applied to other types of businesses as well. The challenges that insurance agents are facing today are similar to the challenges that small business owners in almost any industry also face. Inside, you will find a clear path to survive (and thrive) in this climate of uncertainty. There is no need to operate like a deer in headlights. Knowledge is power, and the more you know about your industry and your customers' needs, the more likely you are to experience compounding success.

Last of all, I don't want to convey concepts that have not been tested in our industry. I stand behind the concepts proven by leaders in lean thinking and have applied them to our organization, My Family Health Insurance.

My Family Health Insurance is a General Agency located in northern Michigan. Throughout this book we share our experiences in applying lean thinking, as well as a few additional concepts of our own. Our hopes are that you find great success in your career in applying the concepts of the Innovative Agent, just as we have.

The Entrepreneurial Renaissance

On the whole, the insurance industry has characteristically been extremely static and predictable. Brokers knew the various insurance offerings inside and out and sold their products from brick and mortar offices all over Main Street, USA. Those who needed insurance visited their local agent, shopped for the products they needed, established a relationship with their agent and left. The strength of his or her relationships was how brokers became established and served as the foundation of their business. The history of the insurance industry is rooted in the philosophy: if you build it, they will come. Do you remember the old Kevin Costner movie from the '90s, *Field of Dreams*? Costner's character was driven by the same philosophy. It paid off for him in spades; and it paid off for insurance brokers too.

The New Normal

Starting an insurance agency is really no different than any other startup venture. The risks and survival rate (one out of ten) are roughly the same as other ventures. Insurance companies that did survive under the old model enjoyed a steady and predictable playing field, until now.

The insurance market has been turned upside down, due largely to the Affordable Care Act. Government regulations are driving the train and infusing several different variables, the likes of which the insurance world has never seen before. For example, there is now a mandated "play or pay" for every adult individual in the country, which means you either buy health insurance or you pay a penalty for not buying it.

Prior to the Affordable Care Act (ACA), insurance companies could operate their business in a relatively unregulated manner, allowing them the freedom to structure agent commissions in a manner that best fit their objectives. But now, the Medical Loss Ratio (MLR), which, under the ACA, requires insurance companies to spend 80% of individual and small group revenue on healthcare and quality improvement efforts and 85% for large group, has significantly impacted what carriers can pay an agent.

To illustrate what this new normal looks like, in Michigan, one of the regional carriers paid a 20% first-year commission written on "individual" business prior to the ACA. Now, this carrier has cut commissions in half. And of course, this is a federal law for all insurance carriers doing business in the health insurance markets. So, reduced commission has become a common problem for health insurance agents across the entire country.

Yet, the bad news doesn't end there. Because of the constraints, insurance companies have no choice other than to compete more aggressively, thus, taking in customers through their call centers, further complicating the problems and costs of acquiring customers in a world of 50% less commission per client.

Just as you might be thinking, "How could this problem become any worse?" it does, in a massive way. The problem is called Healthcare.gov, or more commonly called "The Marketplace." Throughout the year, but more specifically during the Open Enrollment Period, the federal government spends incredible amounts of money through every medium, including calling you at home, telling you to call Healthcare.gov to buy your insurance before time runs out or you will have to pay a penalty. Coincidentally, while working on this book, sitting in my office at home, I received a call from Healthcare.gov encouraging me to get enrolled. I find this quite puzzling since I have never contacted nor purchased insurance through Healthcare.gov.

The point is the creation of new government regulation in the form of ACA has disrupted the health insurance industry. Many agents have flat out left this industry. The remaining agents are at a crossroad and must find new ways of competing or just hang on for as long as they can before giving up.

A similar phenomenon is taking place in the Financial Services

Industry. In November of 2015, the government sponsored a Roth IRA called MyRA. This program is virtually identical to healthcare.gov, except it's designed for retirement planning. As it gains steam in the coming months and years, you can bet that MyRA will be equally as disruptive to financial advisors as healthcare.gov has been to health insurance agents.

As we continue to move forward, the government is getting more and more of a foothold in traditional businesses across industries through laws, regulation and intervention, and it's only going to continue. This scenario has left a lot of individual business owners wondering where to go from here and how to survive this David versus Goliath landscape.

It's Anyone's Game Now

The good news is, with the ever-increasing advances in technology, almost anyone can start or modify a business these days at a very low price. In fact, advances in technology have led to an entrepreneurial renaissance. People are able to do things a lot faster and cheaper than ever before, which has opened the door for small business owners and startup companies. There are more opportunities to buy and more platforms to buy things from; consumer options are literally exploding.

Take a look back to the mid-1980s. Bill Gates and Paul Allen dreamed of a computer on the desks of every home in the country. They disrupted the market by having and achieving that dream. Computers transformed from being huge mainframe monstrosities that took up entire rooms to compact devices that sit on desktops (and laps!).

With technological advances, comes devastation for some. Entire industries have been wiped out. Who has a typewriter these days? What about the people who made the ribbons or repaired the keys on the typewriters? Forget about the people who serviced the mainframes. Those dinosaurs are long gone.

The speed with which technology is advancing is truly dizzying. Think about this: the telephone was introduced in 1876. Thank you, Alexander Graham Bell. The cellular phone was introduced in 1983, which means humanity had to suffer through landline connectivity for a little over a hundred years. Then, just a short nine years later, in 1992, after seeing the cell phone gain popularity (and connectivity through the expansion of cell phone towers), the smartphone was introduced, disrupting the cell phone market for those players that didn't see smartphone technology coming. Shortly thereafter, in 2007, the iPhone came out, revolutionizing the smartphone market, displacing some competitors completely out of the market. Now, year-by-year, new technologies such as phone apps and cloud-based computing has revolutionized the iPhone and other smartphones exponentially!

Now, almost 1.8 billion people around the world use smartphones made by one manufacturer or another. The computing capabilities within these handheld, pocket-sized devices are only increasing and improving. The batteries last longer, the memories are larger, and now of course, with cloud-based storage options coupled with cloud computing, we can run the entire office from the palm of our hands. Essentially, you get the benefits of a high-powered computer with limitless data storage all combined in your smartphone.

The results of these leaps in technology? The marriage of technologies creates new markets, disrupting (or devastating) mature markets, and in general changing the way simply everything in our society is accomplished and/or communicated. Compounding technology has opened the doors for entrepreneurs to jump on the bandwagon. There are so many options available, both in our personal and business lives.

The faster technology evolves, the more affordable it becomes and the larger the potential for the entrepreneur. Many of the cloud-based applications are free, and some of them are even limitless in terms of storage. Evernote is one example, which is a completely free, organizational and productivity app. Most people would never be able to use the massive amount of storage Evernote offers. The reason they are able to offer the app for free is because the price of cloud storage and cloud computing has plummeted exponentially.

Since the depths of the Great Recession of 2008, entrepreneurs are recognizing and exploiting the technology boom. As a result, there has been no better or cheaper time to launch a startup than now. This is why there has been a big spike in new startups. There's a reason that *Shark Tank* is one of the top rated television shows in the country. America cannot get enough of watching budding entrepreneurs share their business ideas so they can be picked apart by the sharks week after week. National, televised exposure to entrepreneurship has only fanned the fire of the phenomenon.

Consumer Shopping Trends

Consumers, like business owners, are quickly becoming more accustomed to new technologies that entrepreneurs are shoving in front of them almost on a daily basis. On some level, the use of technology has become almost second nature. We automatically turn to our laptops, tablets or smartphones when we want to check the price or availability of an item or service. We have become addicted to these technologies in all areas of our lives.

We've seen consumer adaptability to technology in a big way in the insurance industry. People are not intimidated to buy insurance products online, with or without an agent's assistance. Shopping for insurance, filling out enrollment information and making payment, all conveniently done with a smartphone at the whim of the prospect is making a big impact on how consumers purchase insurance.

Because consumers have changed the way they are buying insurance, the perceived need for an insurance agent is drastically reduced. That personalized level of service is not occurring as frequently anymore and neither the consumer nor the agent is the better for it. As the ease of transacting insurance with the smartphone and electronic enrollment programs improves, the agent's value will be minimized more and more. Agents have no choice but to understand what is happening and employ a strategy to use these changes in technologies to their advantage.

Your Prospects Are Getting Busier By the Day

Before we examine some very interesting statistics from the Pew Research Center about the shopping behavior of your prospects, we need to first understand some of the core reasons why people are choosing to buy insurance online instead of in your office.

1. People are busier because of the economy. Since the recession of 2008, the job market just isn't the same. Fewer "good paying" jobs and downsizing is forcing many breadwinners to work two jobs to make ends meet. The same dilemma is happening in business; disruption is forcing businesses to charge less or provide more value in order to acquire and keep customers.

2. People are busier because of new and evolving technologies. Those of you who grew up in the 1970s and 1980s understand where I'm going with this. Life was less complicated back then, way less. Computers were not available to the average person. There was no surfing the Internet, no Internet games, programs, videos and no e-mails to attend to. We didn't have cell phones either. There were less calls, there was no texting and many of the other distractions associated with the smartphone had not yet been invented. And of course, social media as we know it today, wasn't even on the radar.

Fast-forward to today. The pressure is on to constantly respond to the barrage of e-mails, texts, tweets and various other types of communications, taking up what little bit of time you have left in the day.

All of this busyness, combined with technologies that make enrolling in a health insurance plan, a life insurance plan or car insurance plan quick and simple has converged. Now, consumers know where to shop and enroll in insurances of every kind at their convenience, night or day. By acknowledging these trends, you have a better understanding about where you need to meet your prospects. Disrupters already have!

Your Prospects Are Shopping with Technology

Through technology, business owners and consumers across the spectrum are looking at purchasing insurances in a whole new light. Social media alone has gained a considerable amount of traction within the industry. It's no small wonder, considering that demographically diverse age groups are gathering online to talk and share information. Facebook and other social media platforms cannot be ignored. It's all part of the technological shift that is taking place within the cultural landscape. Not having a social media presence could prove to be as devastating as not having a trustworthy website. To stay viable, agents need to take into consideration how information is being shared and get in on the conversation.

The Pew Research Center has conducted extensive research on technology device ownership, as the following charts indicate. The first chart brings awareness to the most commonly used devices, which is a big part of understanding how consumer behavior is connected to technology and helps us make more informed business decisions. Not surprisingly, cellphones (including smartphones) are the most commonly owned devices. The second is a desktop or laptop computer

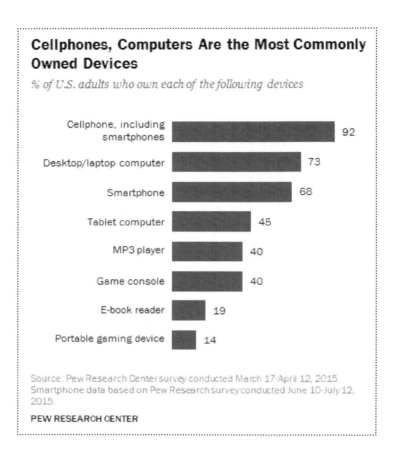

Cellphones, Computers Are the Most Commonly Owned Devices

% of U.S. adults who own each of the following devices

Device	%
Cellphone, including smartphones	92
Desktop/laptop computer	73
Smartphone	68
Tablet computer	45
MP3 player	40
Game console	40
E-book reader	19
Portable gaming device	14

Source: Pew Research Center survey conducted March 17-April 12, 2015. Smartphone data based on Pew Research survey conducted June 10-July 12, 2015.

PEW RESEARCH CENTER

and third is the smartphone.

The second and third charts show just how aggressively people are embracing the technologies offered through smartphones and tablet computers. Soon, they will replace the desktop/laptop if these trends continue.

Now that it's clear that people's use of smartphones and tablets has increased dramatically in recent years, next we

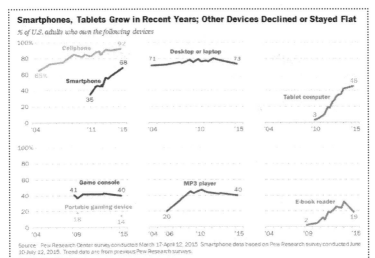

Smartphones, Tablets Grew in Recent Years; Other Devices Declined or Stayed Flat

% of U.S. adults who own the following devices

Source: Pew Research Center survey conducted March 17-April 12, 2015. Smartphone data based on Pew Research survey conducted June 10-July 12, 2015. Trend data are from previous Pew Research surveys.

PEW RESEARCH CENTER

Tablet Owners More Likely to be Younger, More Affluent and Highly Educated

% of U.S. adults who own a tablet computer, e.g. iPad, Samsung Galaxy Tab, Google Nexus or Kindle Fire

U.S. adults	45
Sex	
Men	43
Women	47
Race/ethnicity	
White	47
Black	38
Hispanic	36
Age group	
18-29	50
30-49	57
50-64	37
65+	32
Household income	
<$30K	28
$30K-$49,999	44
$50K-$74,999	51
$75K+	67
Educational attainment	
Less than high school	19
High school	35
Some college	49
College+	62
Community type	
Urban	42
Suburban	50
Rural	37

Source: Pew Research Center survey conducted March 17-April 12, 2015. Whites and blacks include only non-Hispanics. N=959

PEW RESEARCH CENTER

want to look at how many adults are using social media. Why? Because, as the chart on the following page shows, there is an aggressive upward trend in social media use in all age categories. Much like making yourself known in the yellow pages and on the Internet, you need to make your presence known on social media platforms, such as Facebook.

The next chart examines in store shopping habits. Pew Research conducted their study during the 2012 Christmas holiday shopping season to analyze buyer behavior.

According to the Pew Research Center:

Nearly six in ten cell owners used their phone inside a physical store for assistance or guidance on a purchasing decision during the holiday season. In the 30 days preceding our early January 2013 survey (the final weeks of the holiday gift-giving season):

- 46% of cell owners used their phone while inside a store to call a friend or family member for advice about a purchase they were considering.

- 28% of cell owners used their phone while inside a store to look up reviews of a product to help decide if they should purchase it or not.

- 27% of cell owners used their phone while inside a store to look up the price of a product, to see if they could get a better price elsewhere.[2]

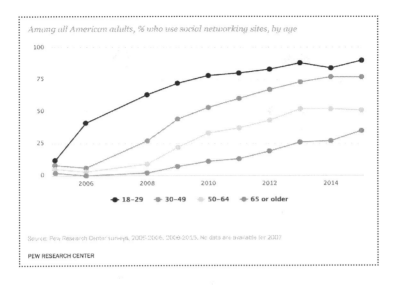

Among all American adults, % who use social networking sites, by age

18-29 • 30-49 • 50-64 • 65 or older

Source: Pew Research Center surveys, 2005-2006, 2008-2015. No data are available for 2007

PEW RESEARCH CENTER

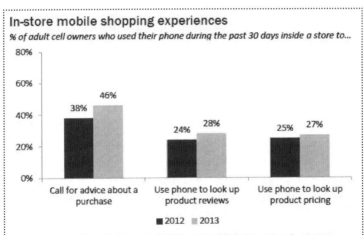

In-store mobile shopping experiences

% of adult cell owners who used their phone during the past 30 days inside a store to...

Call for advice about a purchase: 38% (2012), 46% (2013)

Use phone to look up product reviews: 24% (2012), 28% (2013)

Use phone to look up product pricing: 25% (2012), 27% (2013)

■ 2012 ▥ 2013

Source: Pew Research Center's Internet & American Life Project, Omnibus Survey, January 3-6, 2013. N=1,003 adults ages 18 and older, including 502 interviews conducted on respondent's cell phone. The survey was conducted in English. Margin of error is +/-3.8 percentage points for cell phone owners (n=908).

The chart and the supporting research tell us that people are mobile. They are well informed and their purchasing decisions are based on the best value they can find on the Internet. These behavior trends are not exclusive to holiday shopping patterns. They are a representation of consumer behavior across all industries and all products. No business is immune from these trends!

With the use of social media increasing across all demographics, the insurance agent's exposure if they do something good or bad in the consumer's eyes can go viral. Having and exploiting a good customer acquisition and retention plan is more important than ever.

Let's face the facts: insurance, in the eyes of the consumer, has become just another commodity. The key for agents is to know how people are shopping (on the Internet), with what devices (smartphones) and where they are gathering to discuss their shopping experiences (Facebook). This knowledge will give agents a competitive edge when they are considering how best to re-shape their business model.

Disrupters Among Us

Every industry is experiencing disruption. I'll return to Bill Gates and Paul Allen's computer in every home dream. We know that they achieved market domination for quite a long time as they saw their dream come to fruition. They were able to enjoy long-term profit through a sustainable business plan, while also being keenly aware of the advantages they possessed.

Every business has a bell-shaped curve of existence. This was illustrated through the century-long life of the landline phone. The phone industry was mature and static until it was finally disrupted with the advent of the cell phone. With disruption happening across industries at an ever-increasing speed, it looks like the dream of a computer on every desk and in every home may not be that long-lived. As we saw from the Pew Research, trends show that people are not waiting to go home to their desktop for most of the computer-related tasks.

Disruption is a term that describes the phenomenon of an industry that's been interrupted by unexpected change. (The Introduction of this book includes a full definition). For example, the Affordable Care Act has significantly disrupted the typical health insurance agent's sales process, which translates to lower commissions and less customers.

Not all business models and technologies are disruptive. For example, most people assume that Henry Ford disrupted the automobile industry when he invented the car. The fact is the car was so expensive when it first rolled onto the market that almost no one could afford it. The horse and buggy business carried on, undisturbed for several more decades. Henry Ford didn't invent the car, by the way. He invented the assembly line. (Karl Benz is attributed with inventing the automobile.) When cars started to be mass-produced on the assembly line, the price went way down and suddenly owning one was within reach. Disruption occurs when things become less expensive and more people can afford to buy them.

So what are today's disrupters doing and how can you be

among them? For starters, they are employing a wide array of powerful and low cost technology. They know where and how customers shop for insurance, and they recognize that technology gives them a national audience. Disrupters are true, innovative entrepreneurs. They look for new ways of finding prospects and turning them into clients. Often, they're using off-the-shelf, low-cost technologies to reach a new audience.

I'll use My Family Health Insurance as an example. Much like insurance agents compete against each other, GA's compete against one another as well. Being a new GA of only six months or so, we were well aware of the entrepreneurial renaissance and how we could easily disrupt our market by offering technologies that few, if any other GA's offer. In alignment with our vision, we saw our opportunity to provide free landing pages and websites to agents, with add-on technologies such as direct enrollment portals. It was a home run because we provided a service not offered in our market and we came in at low cost—free!

Once we were armed with the knowledge and ability to create free websites, coupled with direct enrollment portals, the homework on whether this offering would take traction was pretty simple. We did an analysis of the agent community we were targeting and these were some of the highlights of our findings:

- Many agents didn't have a website.

- Other website developers typically charge anywhere from hundreds to thousands of dollars to develop a website. And, many of them charge recurring monthly fees.

💡 An obvious next step after providing a website would be to introduce many other web-centered concepts that are logical "next-steps" after development of the website.

Without question, our proposition of a free website and other technologies disrupted our local GA market. This became clearly evident as we saw a much larger percentage of agents coming onboard after introducing these new technologies to them. Additionally, we were, for the first time, getting new recruits by word of mouth.

Disrupters don't sit around thinking about ways to steal other people's customers. They don't care about your business model or your customers. They are focused on entrepreneurship and innovation. They just want to build an innovative product that offers prospects a convenient and innovative way of buying insurance. Disrupters don't look for incremental growth. They're interested in taking over large segments of the industry very quickly and effectively. Don't be caught off guard. Not knowing about or acknowledging what these disrupters can do to you, your agency and the industry overall could be a very costly mistake.

As mentioned, the insurance industry faces unique challenges because of intense regulation. Government intervention tends to lead to less innovation and over regulation has left us paralyzed. We're typically viewed as being in the dinosaur era, because insurance agents are known for doing things the way they've always been done. We're tested by secret shoppers, HIPAA Compliance through the Department of Labor has added costs, not to mention serious consequences if found non-compliant during an audit, the ever expanding state and federal licensing regulations, the Marketplace, and the list goes on.

In order to break out of the grind, agents have to dig deeper and be aware that there is always going to be something or someone around the corner that could wipe them out. Focus on a lean business model and adopt an entrepreneurial mindset. With innovation comes a piece of the market share and the opportunity to compete in an ever changing landscape.

The Industrial Age vs. The Information Age

I have strong beliefs that the entrepreneurial renaissance we are witnessing isn't just a short-term phenomenon. It's here to stay. I say this because there is plenty of evidence to prove that the U.S., and maybe a few other first-world countries are in transition out of the Industrial age and into the Information Age. In the Information Age, technological breakthroughs will become common place on an ever-increasing speed and scale.

Historically, there are cycles of great progress by mankind that makes the previous cycle obsolete and the new cycle the norm. During the transitions, there is a lot of disruption because the previous paradigms are extinguished as the new paradigms are developing. During these transitions, there are a lot of losers and a few winners that reap incredible wealth. Visionaries not only recognize the transition, but also embrace it and position themselves to be at the front end of the bell curve.

For example, let's look at how mail is delivered to you. Prior to the Industrial Revolution, mail was sent and received on horseback. As we entered the Industrial Age it all started to change. The automobile became common and affordable for everybody. Soon, the U.S. Postal system came into existence, displacing delivery of mail on horseback.

Soon, I believe, we will see Amazon's entrepreneurial vision of delivering products with drones to its customers within 30 minutes of purchase. Their vision is well documented. You can learn more about it by doing a search for "Amazon Prime Air."

It's important that you focus on Information Age sales techniques and technologies as much as possible when searching for innovative ways to connect with your prospects.

In the next five chapters, I am going to lay out the key principles of becoming an Innovative Agent. Much of this model is based on the principles found in Eric Ries', *The Lean Startup* and Ash Maurya's, *Running Lean*. I have added other important elements to their ideas that are crucial and specific to the insurance industry, although they are applicable to many other sales industries as well. Essentially, it is a very simple and straightforward business management model that will help you to rise above the din, reclaim your position in the industry and be profitable. Are you ready?

Entrepreneurship

> *"Anyone who is creating a new product or business under conditions of extreme uncertainty is an entrepreneur whether he or she knows it or not and whether working in a government agency, a venture-backed company, a nonprofit, or a decidedly for-profit company with financial investors."*
>
> — ERIC RIES, THE LEAN STARTUP

Characteristics of an Entrepreneur

It's common to dismiss or overlook the true definition of being an entrepreneur. The tendency is to associate business survival with entrepreneurship, which is not an entirely accurate leap of logic. We've heard the famous statistic before: nine out of ten businesses fail. The business owner of the one out of ten that makes it might think to him or herself, "I survived, so I'm an entrepreneur." The title is used almost as a right of passage, although it does not apply to everyone.

There are other misconceptions associated with the term as well. For example, there are those who think that being an entrepreneur only applies to being a startup. Not so! As Eric Ries, author of *The Lean Startup*, says in his quote at the beginning of this chapter, "Anyone can be an entrepreneur." It's not just for startups; established business owners can be entrepreneurs too, in fact, many of them are! It's important to understand the true definition, as clearly presented above, so you can identify the entrepreneurs within your organization if you don't happen to be one yourself. It is the entrepreneur in your organization who will need to be at the forefront of change in your organization as you employ the principles of the Innovative Agent.

Entrepreneurs are fairly easy to recognize. They're the ones who are shaking things up and questioning everything. They typically wear a lot of hats and challenge the status quo. They say, "Why are we doing it this way? Have we thought about doing it that way? Who says we can't? Let's try it and see!" Or they'll say, "The business model we're using right now stinks. Why are our sales so off the projections?" Entrepreneurs are the odd balls who stand out in a business, either in a leadership role or as a staff member.

In order to succeed with the Innovative Agent business model, you or someone in your organization must be an entrepreneur. Someone must be looking at things through a different lens and from a different perspective. Knowing the definition of being an entrepreneur isn't enough; you need to have one on your team. Just because you own a business or have shares in it, does not mean you're an entrepreneur.

The entrepreneur is willing to take risks, even if failure seems obvious to everyone else around them. Someone needs to be willing to stick their neck out and make bold moves to take the company to the next level. Failure is inevitable. You cannot have success without it. It's not something to be afraid of. Failure is just a part of the game, which is a concept the entrepreneur recognizes at his very core. It doesn't mean the entire business will collapse; it simply means that you have to be willing to test new concepts, not all of which will hit the ball out of the park. To the Innovative Agent, failure isn't seen as failure. Instead, it's an opportunity to learn more about their prospect. By allowing oneself to learn from failure, the Innovative Agent better understands the prospects' wants and needs, which gets him/her one step closer to product fit.

On the other hand, those who are not entrepreneurs have a hard time wrapping their heads around failure and its inevitability. To move the needle in a positive direction and to affect real change, a business must assume some risk. This means trying and testing new concepts. It means recognizing that there are many different ways of connecting your organization to your prospects. The more avenues you pursue, the more likely you are of finding the right one. Some of them will be dead ends, and some of them might lead to a pot of gold. Without trying, and running into those dead ends, you'll never find the pot of gold.

e of your entrepreneur will be to build and test
ions. It takes a person with an entirely fresh and new
it to oversee the process of creation, implementation,
‑‑‑‑‑ and optimizing innovative products or services. You
need someone within your organization who is capable of
thinking the unthinkable. Without an entrepreneur to guide
the organization using the Innovative Agent model, the business
 lacks the vision and dedication to innovate their way to
success and sustainable growth.

Creatures of Habit

People are creatures of habit, which can be a tricky characteristic especially with insurance agents. Most agents are independent and running their businesses out of their home or remote one or two-person offices. There are very few brick and mortar businesses left in our community, so every agent needs to adopt an entrepreneurial mindset. They need to be the chief cook and bottle washer and many of them know that already and are up to the task.

More established agents however, who have been in the business for some time, are more resistant to change. They tend to be more entrenched in their current way of doing things and less apt to embrace risk or shake things up. Usually they are in a place where they are so busy managing day-to-day activities, they struggle to see the forest for the trees. The more entrenched you are in your business and your current way of operating; the more difficult it is to embrace an entrepreneurial mindset.

For those who are experiencing this latter scenario, I have two simple recommendations. Identify the person who is going to lead the entrepreneurial charge within your company and have a frank discussion with them about what their role is going to be. Set them on a crash course to learn everything they can about being an entrepreneur. Everybody learns differently; some prefer reading and some learn more effectively by watching videos.

Whatever the preferred method of learning, there are literally thousands of resources available. The Amazon bookshelf is filled with titles that can be easily located by entering the search terms "entrepreneur" or "startups." There are all kinds of amazing books that can quickly get someone up to speed on what it means to be an entrepreneur today as opposed to 5, 10 or even 15 years ago.

If your entrepreneur prefers video, I refer them to www.thisweekinstartups.com, created by Jason Calacanis. The site has over 600 interviews that include interviews with successful entrepreneurs, book authors and other experts within the field. It's a great place to visit to get a taste of what it's like to be an entrepreneur.

Being an entrepreneur isn't simply a state of being; it's a constant evolution. There are always new ideas and technologies and things are always shifting in the insurance industry. It requires getting into the mindset and understanding the entrepreneurial psyche. Sometimes, entrepreneurial thinking comes down to survival and the characteristics and tendencies can be self-taught.

The insurance industry is not often associated with entrepreneurial thinking as are many industries. We touched on this point earlier, but to reiterate, innovation does not often flourish in an environment that is associated with government regulation. Agents tend to gravitate toward a more traditional mindset, and often they're so buried and overwhelmed, that they behave like a deer in headlights. They know something has to change or they're going to get hit, but they're frozen and they can't get out of their own way.

Validating Your Market Landscape

As an entrepreneur, the starting point to embracing the Innovative Agent business model is to validate the market landscape. To do this, you need to reexamine your company's vision. Once you are in touch with your vision, you can take a step back and analyze your current business model. Every industry will have a different set of questions that need to be examined, but roughly, they will look a little something like this:

- What is working (and just as importantly, not working) in your current business plan?

- What are your competitors doing to beat you at your own game?

- What changes in technology should you be concerned about or use to your advantage?

- What are the buying habits of your prospects and customers?

All business owners need to take a hard look at how they are operating and what is going on around them. Take an objective snapshot of where you are today. Step away from the chaos and the noise of operating a business and assess your approach and systems. One of the key ways to do this is to examine the threats so you can begin to safeguard your business. Comprehensively analyzing your vision and what is happening in your industry has to be your starting point.

For example, with My Family Health Insurance, one of the biggest areas we needed to focus our attention was technology. We had to put some energy into figuring out what kind of cool, cutting-edge technology we could put in front of agents to help them better reach their customers and stand apart from our competition.

A beautiful side perk of focusing on technology first, is that you'll likely stumble onto a solution that can also be used internally. The very same thing that helps you to expand and grow your business can be used to streamline processes that will make you more efficient and lower your operating costs.

What's working in your business model? What's not?

Remember the illustration of the Industrial Age vs. the Information Age. You will want to consider things such as:

♀ What's your business slogan? "We've been in business for 50 years" doesn't resonate with people the way it used to. Your slogan needs to be in alignment with how you want your customers and prospects to perceive you.

- ♀ Are sales and upsells waning? Is your product not getting the attention of prospects the way it used to?

- ♀ Are customer acquisition costs going higher? Conversely, are you retaining customers as long as the industry norm or better?

- ♀ What are your sales demographics? Do you sell more to one group of people than you do others?

There is a plethora of questions you need to ask yourself, so be sure to be thorough.

What are your competitors doing to beat you at your own game?

Insurance has traditionally been the kind of industry where consumers book an appointment with an agent, go down to their office, fill out a bunch of paperwork and are then enrolled in a program. Well, we now know that consumers want convenience above all else. How are your competitors rising to the top of the crop to deliver? For example, are they offering fast and easy enrollment through electronic portals available by smartphone? Pay attention to what others are doing in your field to give the customer what they want, and don't allow yourself to get squeezed out.

Be careful in examining other competitors, you might fall into the trap of trying to copy some of them. There was a business term several decades ago called "benchmarking." Through benchmarking, you would compare what your business practices were in comparison to industry leaders. You would consider your shortcomings and make the needed changes to realign your business to theirs. I recommend that you stay away from that practice today, primarily for one reason. In today's highly competitive environment, the industry leaders you examine are likely disrupters who are highly innovative and practice skills discussed in this book.

Disrupters don't build a "once and done" business model. They are always innovating, testing and iterating to the next level. If you try to duplicate their model, by the time you succeed, they and much of your competition have moved on to the next level, leaving you no further ahead than you were when you started.

What changes in technology should you be using?

It's important to keep in mind that we are only looking at the landscape right now. We're not at the point where we can make assumptions and build products our customers are looking for. But, in the age of technology, you need to know what technologies are available for you to use, as well as identify what technologies your competition is using against you. Here are some ideas:

♀ Go online and look to purchase a product you sell. For example, if you sell life insurance for a living, Google "buy life insurance." You will easily find your biggest competitors in just a few minutes. Sure, you will find cool enrollment portals and other flashy technology that you can't afford to build. But, by doing some looking around, you will surely find similar quoting software available for free that you can personalize with your business name and number! Many GA's and MGA's offer these free direct enrollment portals if you partner with them.

- There are countless free or very low cost technologies available that will not only help you to build new products for your prospects, but also help you operate your business more efficiently and at much less expense. Check out www.Capterra.com. They have more than 300 different categories of software to pick and choose from, again, many of them at no cost!

- Contact a GA (General Agent) or a MGA (Managing General Agent). GA's and MGA's are located throughout the country in just about every state. These entities offer agent solutions for almost any situation. They are oftentimes the "first in" with new, innovative products and processes.

What are the buying habits of your prospects and customers?

In Chapter 4 we will go into detail about your new business model, which is based on continuous discussions with your customers and prospects, so you can better understand and meet their needs. Until then, learn more about them on a larger scale:

- Gather information from resources about people's shopping habits, such as the Pew Research Center, trade publications and other sources.

◊ Collect information from the insurance companies you work with. For example, a regional health insurance company was recently discussing how important the agent community was to them; 60% of their new business is placed through them. It stands to reason that the other 40% of their business came from their call centers or from Healthcare.gov. It is this second group of prospects you want to learn more about so you can ultimately provide a solution for them to buy their insurance through you.

The bottom line is, entrepreneurs are everywhere. In order for the entrepreneur to apply an innovative concept to grow your business, there has to be a clear understanding of the landscape in order to get started.

THREE

Specialization

The Riches Are in the Niches

You've heard that old saying, "the riches are in the niches?" Or more commonly, "A Jack of all trades is a master of none." Essentially, no one business can be all things to all people. You will have a far higher chance of success if you focus on one thing and do it extremely well. Specialization is the name of the game, even in the insurance industry.

As mentioned in Chapter 2, one of the best video resources for entrepreneurs is http://thisweekinstartups.com. At the very end of one of my favorite episodes (#423), the host Jason Calacanis asks *Shark Tank*'s Mark Cuban, "What is the one piece of advice you would give to entrepreneurs today? What do they need to know to be successful?"

Off the top of his head, Mark rattled off 5 key points for entrepreneurs to take into consideration.[3]

1. Everybody has ideas. Ideas are easy. Everybody has them.

When using the Innovative Agent business model, you'll come up with hundreds of ideas. That's the easy part.

2. It's a grind. You just have to keep to grinding.

Entrepreneurs don't work 9 to 5 office hours. It's not who they are. They are passionate about their vision and their business. It's hard to pull an entrepreneur away from work. They are relentless and work long hours, including weekends. They're almost never satisfied with the "status quo." If you are truly passionate about your business, you not only understand what Mark Cuban was saying, but you embrace it as part of your life.

If you aren't passionate about your business, you're most likely not going to, as Mark puts it, "grind" relentlessly and tirelessly. And if you're not passionate about your business, you may want to consider exiting now (voluntarily) rather than later (at a much reduced valuation).

3. If you don't know your product or service and industry better than anybody else, whoever does is going to kick your ass.

This point is the key to what this chapter is all about: specialization. As discussed, disruption is coming from every direction. For most agents, trying to sell multiple lines of insurance simultaneously is a practice in futility. For example, I commonly see agents selling health insurance products in the "under age 65" market as well as the Medicare market. Granted, this is doable, but there aren't enough hours in the day to specialize in both. Failure to specialize prevents you from becoming a leader in either area of expertise, mitigating serious growth opportunities and making you very vulnerable to disruption. Our industry is no different than any other; you cannot be a jack-of-all-trades but a master of none.

4. You always have to say to yourself: If I were competing with me, how would I kick my own ass?

Even the best businesses have weaknesses that could lead to their demise in one way or another. As a practice, you should always take a step back, look at your business model and explore ways that it could be disrupted. Believe me, many of your competitors already are. Then, consider what contingency plans you would put in place in the event that your business is disrupted.

5. There are no short cuts. You've just got to grind it out and keep on grinding.

Even though Mark didn't say so specifically, what he's really screaming from the mountaintop is, "Specialize!"

There's No Better Time Than the Present

Specialization is an important part of the Innovative Agent model. It affords you the time and the resources needed so you can most effectively grow your business. Here are the top seven reasons why you need to specialize.

1. *Regulations.* Everyone in the insurance industry is familiar with the regulations that govern us. It becomes much more complex when we work in two or more lines of business. Adhering to regulations in multiple lines is difficult, time consuming and leaves us open for errors that can lead to litigation.

2. HIPAA. Failure to maintain a good privacy program can be catastrophic if an event happens and you are audited. Not understanding or having the resources to maintain a compliant system in two or more lines of insurance is easy to do.

3. *Training / certifications.* Training requirements are anything but static in our industry. It seems like there is a never-ending increase in regulations, resulting in more and more comprehensive training requirements. Being compliant in multiple lines of insurance is a huge drain on time and resources.

4. *Resources.* Besides additional resources needed to meet the other six points, there are countless other time consuming complexities, such as internal training, advertising, supplies, carrier, client and prospect communications. The list just goes on.

5. *Lower Commissions.* Commissions are decreasing in many lines of insurance and the likelihood of this continuing is quite likely. Earning less commission on each sale when

you are already stretched thin in resources and time makes a bad situation much worse. When you are paid less and have no extra hours in the day to make up the losses in additional sales, something has to give.

6. *Expertise.* It is never fun losing business to a competitor because they were more on their game than us. As a matter of fact, it's painful. It not only hurts the pride but it hurts the bank account. When you sell in more than one line of insurance, this is what you can expect. Lack of expertise makes you average. You can't break out of "average" unless you free up time to specialize.

7. *Focus.* Not specializing means you're not focusing. By focusing you will see business from a whole new light. Less regulation, less training, and less stress on your limited resources gives you time to get to know your prospects, to employ innovative solutions, and to achieve the vision of your business.

In the Industrial Age, as a business, you could ignore your problems for much longer periods than you can now. Today, if you act like an ostrich by sticking your head in the sand for very long, you will find yourself out of business. Making up your mind to specialize, if not today, but soon, will lead you to higher ground in your career.

Of course, there are exceptions to the rule. There are very large and innovative agencies throughout the U.S. that are very successful in many lines of business. They have seen their success and will continue to see success because they wisely divide their company in segments, putting leaders in each area to carry out the tasks needed to meet the demands of the company's vision.

The Painful Road to Specialization

From our inception around the beginning of 2014 until late summer of 2015, My Family Health Insurance had a very lofty agent recruitment goal in both the "individual—under age 65" market as well as the "individual—Medicare market."

During this time, and with recruits coming in almost weekly, we were finding ourselves maximizing all of our resources. We were offering free websites to all agents but finding ourselves very weak on contracting and servicing the Medicare agents. We found ourselves in a position where we couldn't provide the Medicare agents the high level of commitment and service we were providing the < 65 agents.

We took a look at the over age 65 market and gave some thought as to how we could make it as successful as the under age 65 segment. We knew we didn't have enough manpower to support both, and we lacked the resources to hire additional people. We were also concerned about providing the level of expertise and support our Medicare agents deserved. To pretend that we could, was simply intellectually dishonest. We recognized that the over 65 market was bogging us down and we weren't able to deliver in a way that was in alignment with our model, let alone our vision.

Additionally, we were not getting the GA contracts we wanted.

This was due largely to the fact that we didn't have large enough of a Medicare agent base to warrant higher commission structures to pass on to the agents. We were expending equal or more time trying to grow the under 65 agent onboarding simultaneously. This meant that we were not executing the way we wanted to be. Every new agent we brought in on the Medicare side just increased the burden on us internally. Our growth model was sufficient but we weren't doing the agents justice.

As a team, we made the decision to partner with a competitor *who was an expert* in the over age 65 market. The lost opportunity was a painful one but we understood that it would be several years before we had the resources to serve that market. In the meantime, we could still benefit from a relationship with the experts in that field. We still provide the over age 65 agents with websites, give them their value add and let them know that we're here, but for the day-to-day support, we handed them over to our new partner.

Benefits of Specialization

From that day forward, we were able to get back on track with the onboarding of our under age 65 agents. This meant we were able to optimize the successes that we were experiencing in that market and get ourselves better positioned for scaling the business by optimizing our product offering in the upcoming years. All in all, it's been a win-win.

Business owners sometimes need to make tough or uncomfortable decisions to move ahead. We saw that we were putting resources into the Medicare market but ultimately we were underserving it. To compound matters, we weren't doing justice to our bread and butter market either. We were in an embarrassing and painful position. As hard as it was to let go of a market segment, we knew it was the right thing to do. In making the decision to specialize exclusively in the under 65 market, all of our agents would be well taken care of. Plus, we had peace of mind knowing that we made the decision with their best interests at heart.

Our agents appreciated the choice that we made. The goodwill that our decision to partner with another GA—who could better serve the Medicare market, so that we in turn could better serve the under 65 agents—opened the door for a referral business. Now when an agent calls us, if they happen to be in the Medicare field, we can say, "Listen, we can build you a free website if you partner with us and we'd like to connect you with another agency who can better serve your specific needs." It might sound crazy, but because of this partnership, every time we make a referral to our partner GA, we get an override on the business.

If you're an insurance agent and you're open to specialization, I can promise, you'll be having the same conversation with yourself. You'll be the one saying, "Why didn't I do this sooner?"

If you're an agent who works in two different markets and you see the need to let go of one so you can specialize, there are a few things you can do to ease the transition. Consider talking to some insurance professionals whom you trust to take over the weaker of your two markets. This is truly where the rubber meets the road, and the benefits far out-weigh the pain of letting go.

There is the opportunity to split commissions with the agent you refer the business to, which is quite common within the insurance industry. In that case, you're not only compensated, but you'll find that other doors will open for you too. You've freed up some precious time and manpower to specialize in the area in which you really thrive. You can optimize the resources you have at your disposal because you'll be functioning as the master of one instead of the jack of many. Split commissions allows you to build a solid and long-term income stream through business referrals. Sure, it's not the whole commission, but something is better than nothing! Your referral agent in many ways becomes an extension of your own business.

The best and most rewarding side effect of specialization, however, is knowing your clients are in the best possible hands. When you specialize, you can focus solely within your "sweet spot," prospect for the best customers for your expertise and function within your core knowledge base. What a great model to make additional income and help to support a new and innovative mindset. Everybody's happy and it's just the beginning!

Vision

The Landscape, Revisited

As agents in the insurance business, we are facing several daunting issues. I've covered many of them in Chapter 1, but it's worth reiterating some of the main factors. The landscape of our industry has shifted dramatically in just the past five to ten years. We live in different times now, and the old management systems that prescribed lengthy business plans and the "build it and they will come" philosophy are outdated. To remain competitive in today's world, you cannot rely on a static platform. Stability and predictability are the casualties of change and with their departure; we must adopt new models and strategies for growth and prosperity.

In recognizing the need for a new model, we accept that the old systems are no longer valid. Something needs to give. If we don't start doing things differently, the other players in the market are going to be eating our lunch. Agents are being devoured like a pack of gazelles while the disrupters dominate the industry. We need to stop letting circumstances control us and instead control our circumstances.

The Innovative Agent model will equip insurance agents across all industries to meet the formidable challenges that we face today and in the future. We are not experts in the field of change management or the economies of scale, but we have experienced incredible success in applying the principles of lean thinking to My Family Health Insurance.

We want to share our conviction, experience and successes in applying lean thinking principles insurance agents need to apply in order to meet the challenges discussed in this book so that they too can enjoy the successes in competing effectively in the Information Age.

The Innovative Agent model is a combination of concepts introduced by authors Eric Ries (*The Lean Startup*), Ash Maurya (*Running Lean*) and Clayton Christensen (*The Innovator's Dilemma*). Their collective proven and tested concepts have contributed immeasurably to the entrepreneurial renaissance that we are experiencing today. I've also included a few principles that I've discovered on my own through trial and error in the development of My Family Health Insurance.

This model is designed to help you quickly identify the products and processes that are working for your business. A large part of this involves speaking with your customers about what they want. Think of it as if you were designing a new toy. First, you would talk to a collection of kids and find out what they want. Then you build the toy according to their feedback and specifications. They're the ones who will be clamoring for their parents to buy them the toy. They know what they want above anyone else. You wouldn't want to build or try to sell a product that your customers don't want. This process of build, measure and learn engages your customers and designs products specifically for their needs.

Groupthink

Before getting started, it's important that we address a problem that can stand in the way of progress. The problem is groupthink:

> *Groupthink is a psychological phenomenon that occurs within a group of people, in which the desire for harmony or conformity in the group results in an irrational or dysfunctional decision-making outcome. Group members try to minimize conflict and reach a consensus decision without critical evaluation of alternative viewpoints, by actively suppressing dissenting viewpoints, and by isolating themselves from outside influences.[4]*

Each year, agents in each insurance industry gather together for various group events, such as award banquets, carrier meetings, association meetings and so on. My observation (in my area of expertise, health and life) is that almost the same players show up year after year to these events. Not much changes except the addition of grey hair and reading glasses slung around their necks. Not as many younger agents are coming into the industry, as one would expect.

It's easy to think "this is the way we've always done this" or "If it ain't broke, don't fix it," especially when the way you have done business spans multiple decades. Making the changes needed to implement this model will really rub against groupthink. Be cognizant that groupthink could derail you if you allow it to take precedence over the principles we will be exploring.

The Innovative Agent's Roadmap

"Startups also have a true north, a destination in mind; creating a thriving and world-changing business. I call that a startup's vision. To achieve that vision, startups employ a strategy, which includes a business model, a product roadmap, a point of view about partners and competitors, and ideas about who the customer will be. The product is the end result of this strategy."

— ERIC RIES, THE LEAN STARTUP

The following chart depicts the simplistic business model used by the Innovative Agent. You have a **vision** of what your business does, what its goals are and where you want to take it. You will build upon your vision by offering a **product** that your customers desire. And, you will deliver the product to your customer using a **strategy.**

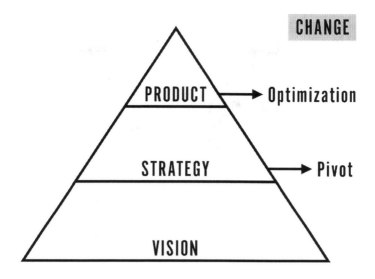

Vision

You have a goal for your business that translates into a vision. Though your vision may not be to deliver one simple product or process, it can't be as vague as "to sell insurance products to my prospects." If you don't have a clearly defined and focused vision, you need to develop it clearly and document it. Keep it in front of your team at all times. If the team doesn't understand the vision, the resulting consequences will be distraction, confusion and a waste of valuable resources.

Although you will learn to experiment on new products and processes continuously, it is the entrepreneur's responsibility to keep those activities in alignment with the vision.

For example, My Family Health Insurance has a vision of exponential growth of revenue through two channels:

1. Agent over-rides generated through agent recruitment

2. Agent education through various channels

There are many different ways of generating income through these two channels, but we choose only a few and work tirelessly on those two areas. Sure, we are walking away from "no brainer" opportunities, but if we don't have a laser-focus on what we do best, we will become diluted, earning a little income from a lot of opportunities. Large income potential only comes through specialization.

Product

Strategy is the process by which you deliver a product to the end user, your customer. So, it makes sense to first know the product and then determine what internal processes are needed to deliver the product to your customer.

It's tempting to skip over this topic because of the appearance of the obvious. Insurance agents may think that the product they offer is an insurance policy. It's not. Your product is *how you connect with prospects* in order to sell them an insurance product.

Again, using My Family Health Insurance as an example:

In 2015, the product we used to connect with a large segment of agents was a free website. This was a no-brainer considering:

1. The vast majority of agents we were reaching out to either didn't have a website or their website was outdated.

2. We had the capability of creating free websites for agents at an exceptionally low cost to us.

3. We knew there was an overwhelming need and exploited it with great success in alignment with part of our vision— agent recruitment.

In 2016, we are still offering free websites as one of our products. However, we are adding many free or low-cost value-added products for agents as an incentive to work with us as their GA. Why?

As you will soon learn, the Innovative Agent is constantly applying a Build, Measure, Learn, feedback loop to make their product continuously better. Here at My Family Health Insurance, we know our competition very well. If we didn't employ continuous improvement to our product, a competing GA who also offers free websites could easily disrupt us overnight.

Likewise, through the Build, Measure, Learn, feedback loop, we know our customers and prospects very well. We are in front of them constantly. We don't just "listen" to them when they have something to say. We proactively interview them, searching for ways of improving our product offering to them while also looking at new, innovative ways to get to the next level.

Look at your product to see how effectively you are connecting with your prospects. Here are some insights on how to get started:

1. Are you meeting your customers where they shop? Explore how prospects enroll in your products with your competitors. Talk with lost customers to see how and where the competitor met them and enticed them away from you.

2. Do you make it easy for prospects to connect with you? Remember, your prospects are busy. How many barriers do your prospects need to go through to buy an insurance policy from you as compared to leaders in your market?

3. Are you making it easy for customers to stay with you? This seems out of context but it's very important. If you build a practically barrier-free product for your prospects, why would you not include, as a selling point just how barrier-free it is to renew with you? Kill two birds with one stone; customer retention is a key factor in your growth strategy!

Strategy

I have mentioned that your strategy is the process by which you deliver a product to your customer. While this is accurate, it's not the whole picture. Your strategy is comprehensive. It includes things such as:

- ♀ Who your competitors are and how you position yourself to compete against them

○ What's happening with industry and government regulation that might have an impact on your business

○ What trends are working with and against your business and how to deal with them

○ What are the strengths and weaknesses of your team and what should you do to make your team stronger and more efficient

For each business, the strategy varies. And, because of changes in all of the variables internally and externally, the strategy will change from time to time.

The Importance of Innovation

The Innovative Agent builds, tests and optimizes products in alignment with his/her vision. The resulting product fits into one of four different types of innovation. Before outlining the types of innovation you could choose from to build your product, I want to emphasize the importance of innovation in your business. Though I'm not a big fan of cliché's, I do want to bring to your attention a quote you have probably heard many times over—"Innovate or Die."

Innovation has to be at the core of what you do. With disrupters and quickly changing technologies always knocking on your door, you have no other choice other than to innovate. Though your business can survive without innovative product offerings, it likely won't survive much longer or you will find yourself, as Eric Ries puts it, "walking in the land of the living dead."

Your goal is not just innovation, but disruptive innovation. Your entrepreneur needs to make bold moves by making leap of faith assumptions about what your customers want and then test it out. That means you don't want to apply incremental innovation, taking what you do today and only improving on it. This approach totally dismisses the concepts behind the Innovative Agent. We will discuss incremental innovation in greater detail a little later.

Breakthrough innovation refers to a radical breakthrough in a product or service, usually in response to totally unmet needs of the customer. It could come about as a result of combining several different products into one new product or service. Examples of such innovation are ATM machines, the iPad and online shopping. All three of those inventions served to irreversibly disrupt their respective industries.

Another example of a company utilizing breakthrough innovation is Zenefits. Launched in early 2013, Zenefits uses cloud-based software to offer HR services and group health benefits across the U.S. In just a few years, they have grown to well over 10,000 group-clients, nation-wide. The company's numbers are simply astronomical.

In January 2015, Zenefits announced that it had revenue of approximately $20 million in 2014, twenty times the corresponding figure in 2013, despite offering its platform to users for free and making all of its money from commissions charged to insurers for being the insurance broker. In April 2015, the company announced that in March 2015, it had added more clients than it had added in its previous 15 months of operation.[5]

Sustaining innovation is an incremental improvement on a current product or service in response to customer needs, such as second or third generation changes. An example would be Apple's second-generation iPad, the iPhone 6 Plus or same-day dry cleaning. It's taking a product and making it better, usually due to customer feedback. Sustaining innovation could also include cost reduction as part of the additional offerings through product and/or process modifications.

My Family Health Insurance has only been around since 2014, so we are a very young organization. When we first started out, our product was simply a free landing page located on the map of Michigan (by county) on our home page. Our value add was to offer visibility to our agents, by county, and we included a brief bio and headshot of each agent. We didn't know that we had the capability to build out full-scale sites for our agents, but they were thrilled with the landing pages. In fact, they absolutely loved them!

In 2015, we figured out a way that we could optimize our product by rolling out full-scale websites at a very low cost. We also discovered that we could add direct enrollment portals for free so that our agents' clients could easily sign up for dental, vision, disability and other insurances. Without question, *Sustaining Innovation* was the type of innovation we employed for this product.

New market innovation applies to the repurposing of a product to suit a different market need. An example of this is Arm & Hammer baking soda, which was used in baking for decades. More recently, it has been discovered that the same product is effective at eliminating odors in a refrigerator.

In the insurance world, another example is prescription drugs. Pharmaceutical companies that bring new drugs to market get the privilege of higher pricing as a "brand name" until the patent runs out. At that point, the drug becomes available to the public through any competitor, as a generic.

However, if the drug manufacturer can find another benefit for the drug through clinical trials, the drug can fall into another patent-protected period, preventing the generic drug from going to market by the competitors and thus, compounding profits.

Disruptive innovation, coined by Clayton Christensen in his book *Innovator's Dilemma*, occurs when a prohibitively expensive or complicated product is transformed into a simpler product that can be afforded by the masses. Some examples include:

Rail transport disrupted by the automobile:

The quickest and most efficient way to transport people and products in the late 1800s was by trains, including streetcars such as those still in operation in San Francisco. Through the vision of Henry Ford, mass production helped to bring the cost of automobiles down low enough so the average person could afford to purchase one.

Icebox disrupted by refrigerators:

In the early 1900s, most households owned an icebox, which was merely a non-mechanical insulated box that held ice in order to keep food cool. The icebox became obsolete upon the arrival of the refrigerator.

Longbows disrupted by firearms:

Prior to the invention of the gun, the primary method for harvesting big game animals was by bow and arrow. As crude as it was, there was no other efficient way of harvesting these animals.

The Insurance Industry's dilemma with Enrollment Portals

Now that we've looked at the various types of innovation from which you'll derive your product, it's important that we further review the importance of not employing incremental innovation as your innovative solution for product / market fit. There's no better illustration than the new and innovative technology that is sweeping the insurance industry: electronic direct enrollment portals.

Electronic direct enrollment portals (EDEPs) are used for just about every insurance product available: dental, vision, health insurance, life insurance, disability, voluntary plans, tele-doctor, and the list goes on. The technology is simple and straightforward. Search for the product you want, including the provider network (if applicable), enter your personal information, including your contact information, and then fill out your payment method using your credit card. Hit submit and you're done.

These portals have revolutionized the way that people enroll because:

1. Agents can quickly and efficiently take a client through the enrollment process

2. EDEPs give the agent the lowest cost option for enrolling a prospect.

3. Consumers visiting the agent's website can enroll themselves without the assistance of the agent, yet, the agent gets credit/commission.

4. Insurance companies see a lower cost of customer acquisition.

My Family Health Insurance recognized the advantages of this new technology and in turn, offers a wide variety of these portals that recruited agents can have added to their free website at no cost. Surprisingly, after providing countless portals to our agent partners for roughly a year now, we have found that, overwhelmingly, agents rarely use them. With even the lowest initial projections of agent utilization of these portals, agent use of them turned out to be just a fraction of the expectation.

Further, I was one of a small number of agents invited to test out a new EDEP with advanced capabilities with a regional carrier in the summer of 2015. My understandings are that this new EDEP isn't seeing the successes they were looking for, even with the advanced "bells and whistles" they offer as compared to other EDEPS.

This dilemma is an example of incremental innovation. As good as the EDEP technology is, insurance companies and TPA's (third party administrators) aren't seeing agents embracing this technology the way that they perceived it would. Taking a business model and tweaking it is not the type of innovation the Innovative Agent will want to employ. It only leads to dead ends.

After having read this book and looking back to this illustration of agents not connecting with the EDEPS, you will easily see what the problem is. Insurance carriers and TPA's failed to *first* take the concept to their customers (insurance agents) and ask them the simple question: "If we were to build this for you, would you use it?" They failed to interview and apply a "build, measure and learn" feedback loop that would reveal the problem of agent disconnect, so they could ultimately employ a product that the agent perceives as a "must have." For today, "close, but no cigar." For the insurance companies or TPA's that want to go back to the drawing board and employ the principles shared in this book, great rewards are just around the corner.

Building Your Product

The very first challenge for an entrepreneur is to take an assumption, a hypothetical product that's in alignment with the vision of the company, and test the validity of the assumption through interviews with prospects. This activity is a radical shift away from traditional management practices.

Traditional management approach of launching a product

or service, which is still used by many businesses yet today, works something like this: Concept, R&D, test, modify, fill warehouses and store shelves with product, and then see if the customer will buy the product. This process can take several years and incredible amounts of money. No wonder 9 out of 10 business startups fail!

The Innovative Agent model deviates dramatically from the traditional approach of building and launching a product or service. The Innovative Agent first wants to know if there is a product fit. This is done by asking three questions:

- Do I have a problem worth solving?

- Is the product I want to build something my customers actually want?

- If I were to build it and charge customers for it, would they buy it?

For example, with My Family Health Insurance, we did have a problem worth solving (agent online visibility). We know that the product (websites) is definitely something our prospective agents want. If we were to sell websites to our agent partners instead of give them away for free, would they pay? Had we charged a fee for website development, would have we recruited as many agents?

The goal is to build a product and then build a business around it by systematically testing to see if it's a product the customer wants. The product is referred to as a minimal viable product (or MVP). It's the most stripped down product that you can put in front of people who are truly interested. If they want to buy that product from you, and if you can build a business around it, then you have your system.

About Your MVP (Minimal Viable Product)

"The MVP is that version of the product that enables a full turn of the Build-Measure-Learn loop with a minimum amount of effort and the least amount of development time."

— ERIC RIES

The MVP has just enough features that it's attractive to early adapters: the people who are willing to test your product and provide you with feedback. However, the MVP should not have too many features which could expose the entrepreneur to increased risk if the product is a failure.

Building a product at the lowest possible cost in the least amount of time allows the entrepreneur the opportunity to pivot quickly and at lowest cost if the MVP has no traction. This concept is the reverse of the traditional management example we talked about earlier. Instead of taking years to develop a product, you bring a MVP to your early adapters and test it quickly for traction. If it's going to fail, you want it to fail quickly, ultimately saving time, money and resources.

The speed with which new products are introduced to the

marketplace is one of the elements characteristic of our times. Products are coming out faster, the market is disrupted more frequently, and entrepreneurs do not have years and piles of money to burn through for a concept or product that is simply not going to work.

As mentioned, the MVP is used to test out bold assumptions, not just incremental improvements to a current product. This is particularly important for an insurance agent; your decisions and behaviors need to **be bold**. At My Family Health Insurance, we made a gutsy move by saying, "We're willing to offer every agent in the state of Michigan a free website if you come on board with us." The feedback from early adopters were a thumbs up, but we really didn't know how strong the response from the agent community would be, considering the limitations on our resources.

This approach has proven to be far more effective than saying to ourselves, "We've been in business for twenty years and we're just going to continue along with business as usual."

In 2014, My Family Health Insurance developed an MVP to help us, in alignment with our vision, gain a strong competitive advantage in recruiting agents. Our MVP was built to showcase our offering; a free landing page that included features commonly seen on a website, such as an About Us section, Services and Contact information. We hosted the landing pages on the My Family Health Insurance website, offering visitors the opportunity to connect with a "My Family Health Insurance agent partner." We approached our agents, in advance, and asked them if they would utilize this product.

The product was met with resounding enthusiasm and we proceeded to recruit and build out websites at a furious pace.

For us, this was the ideal MVP as it was extremely minimal. All we had to do was create simple "example websites," let them know we could adjust to their preferences and then build it out.

In our case, there were three main components and costs associated with rolling out the product. We excluded labor costs because the landing pages were built by two of the business owners.

1. A digital map of Michigan on our homepage (http://www. myfamilyhealthinsurance.com/agent-look-up) showing outlines of each of the counties in the state. The map is a plug-in we purchased for a one-time cost of $60.

2. Spring boarding off of our previously acquired, zero-cost website builder, we added website hosting for only $275 per year. We were able to create almost unlimited landing pages or websites at a constantly decreasing average cost for every agent recruited! The landing pages or websites were then assigned to the counties where the agents are located.

3. We created an advertisement, which we placed at the top of our homepage saying, "Let us connect you with a local, trusted My Family Health Insurance agent."

The MVP was a success! We took a conceptual and undeveloped product (website) and were able to provide it to prospective agents as close to zero cost as possible. While recruiting agents with our new product, we continued with our interviews and searched for answers on how best we could optimize our product moving forward. Our goal is to expand innovative technologies to our current and prospective agent partners, utilizing the Build, Measure, Learn feedback loop concept I'll explain next.

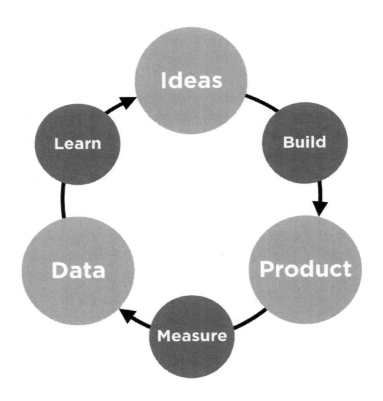

The Build, Measure, Learn Feedback Loop

The Build, Measure, Learn feedback loop (BML) originated with Eric Ries, author of *The Lean Startup*, and is the core focus of the Innovative Agent business model. As Mark Cuban said in his interview with Jason Calacanis, the product is the easy part. Anyone can come up with ideas; it's the testing and assessing of their validity and value that separates the good ideas from the bad.

The BML feedback loop is used to help your team focus on turning ideas into products, measure prospect reactions, and then determine whether to pivot or persevere. This process is repeated as many times as necessary until you get adequate product/market fit.

Learning about your prospect is at the heart of this process. If you're going to fail, you want to fail quickly so you waste as little time, money and resources as possible. Equally, the Innovative Agent sees failure much differently than the average businessperson. Failure is seen as a big positive. Failure tells you what doesn't work. Learning what doesn't work is very important information because it gets you closer to the solution of understanding what your customer wants!

Applying the Build, Measure, Learn Feedback Loop

Step 1: Build Your MVP

Your goal is to take your MVP through the BML feedback loop as quickly as possible while achieving maximum learning for the least amount of effort. Though your MVP should be considered the smallest product imaginable, your MVP doesn't have to be your product at all.

An example is the well-known story about Dropbox's three-minute explainer video MVP. It describes the product functionality to early adopters, even though the product had not yet been completely built. After launching the video, Dropbox saw an increase from 5,000 to 75,000 signups overnight.

Another example is the free websites offered by My Family Health Insurance to prospective agents. We offered a concept of a free website (MVP), and delivered a personalized website loaded with electronic direct enrollment portals to those agents that partnered with us.

One of the most commonly used MVPs is a landing page. You present your MVP on a landing page and e-mail it to a large number of prospects to measure feedback. Quite often, the MVP hasn't even been built.

You can learn more about building quick, inexpensive, and powerful MVPs at: http://thenextweb.com/dd/2014/11/12/15-ways-test-minimum-viable-product/#gref

Step 2: Present Your MVP to Early Adopters

Early adopters are those potential customers you are looking for feedback from as you introduce your MVP through the BML feedback loop. They are happy and eager to learn about your new product and aren't hesitant to tell you what they think about it, even when it is flawed.

For example, do you remember in the early days of the iPhone? People lined up for blocks to get their hands on one. Those people were early adopters. They hadn't seen or used an iPhone ever before, but they couldn't wait to try one and give feedback.

You selectively choose your early adopters. They could be customers or prospects. Either way, they need to be people who are open to interviews and testing new things. Be sure to get a good mix of people. For example, if you only interview millennials, you will garner only what is most important to them. This will lead to product bias and lower success rates as other age categories may not see the product as a solution for their needs.

It's important that you don't run into common pitfalls during the interviewing process with early adopters, such as:

1. As the entrepreneur, you are excited about the vision you have of great success when customers line up to buy your product. As a result, it's too easy to fall in love with your MVP. When this happens, you could find yourself trying to *sell* your product rather than trying to *learn* about your product.

2. You have to know the correct questions to ask your early adopter or you risk getting the wrong feedback. Ask open-ended questions such as:

Q What do you think of this product?

Q Would you ever use this product?

Q Does this product solve your problem?

Through the interviewing process, try to learn more about what motivates them, what their needs are, and other important characteristics of who your customer really is.

In the early adopter interviews, you will identify product/market fit. Product/Market Fit is the degree to which a product satisfies a strong market demand.[6] The data you collect from early adopters in attempting to determine product/market fit is subjective. There are commonly used metrics to determine product/market fit but ultimately, it's up to you as to whether you should continue the experimentation through additional cycles of the BML feedback loop (persevere) or develop another product (pivot) and start all over again.

Marc Andreessen was the first person to use the term product/market fit. Explore what the concept means by reading Marc, Sean Ellis and Ash Maurya's publications. Product/market fit is not a complex concept, but it's important to understand, as opposed to making an assumption that could result in failure.

Last of all, there is a difference between product/market fit and product/solution fit you should do your homework on. Your goal is to find those prospects that desire your product, as a "must have," instead of just seeing it as one of many "solutions" they could choose from.

Step 3: Pivot or Persevere?

Now that you've interviewed several early adopters, analyze the data you've collected to see if you have product/market fit. In most cases, it's likely too early to tell. A commonly used metric to determine product/market fit is called "The 40% Rule," which states that if at least 40% of surveyed customers/prospects consider your MVP a "must have," then you have achieved product/market fit.

What if only 25% of your early adopters think your product is a "must have"? Do you just give up? In general, no. *Persevere* by modifying your product and interview the adopters again. If you continue to gain traction, continue repeating the BML feedback loop in search of a final product that gives you the product/market fit you are searching for.

On the other hand, if fewer than 25% of early adopters say your product is a "must have," and you are unable to get more traction through additional cycles of the BML feedback loop, then you need to *pivot*. You pivot when you have come to the realization that your product is not what your prospects want. Remember, this decision is also subjective. Only you can determine when it's time to pivot. If you need to pivot, go back to the drawing board and develop a new assumption, a new leap of faith, and a new product to introduce to early adopters, and always using the BML feedback loop.

There are two things the entrepreneur needs to remember when making a pivot:

1. Though you are starting with a new product, you now know more about your prospects than you ever have before. Use this data to guide your decisions when developing your new product.

2. No matter how many products are developed, the entrepreneur is responsible for ensuring that all products are in alignment with the vision of the company. Alignment is a precursor to success.

Now that we understand the nuts and bolts of what's involved in applying the BML feedback loop, let's take a simplistic look at how it applies in the following example. A life insurance agent wants to launch a new product.

1. The life insurance agent develops a one-of-a-kind innovative product that makes purchasing life insurance fast, easy and convenient. A product that the life insurance agent strongly believes will drastically increase sales and perhaps even disrupt the insurance sales market significantly.

2. Next, the life insurance agent develops a business model needed in order to deliver the product. That's the **build** part of the build-measure-learn loop. The life insurance agent has to build a business process around the product.

3. Then, the life insurance agent interviews early adopters to see if this product, the MVP, is something they perceive as a "must have." If applicable, would they pay for it? All of the questions asked during the interviewing process is what the insurance agent wants to **measure**.

4. The life insurance agent determines how to process early adapter feedback, which is the **learn** part of the process.

5. The life insurance agent repeats step 2 and 3 as many times as necessary to determine if there is enough early adopter interest. If there isn't enough interest, **pivot**.

6. Repeat the process as needed to launch the product.

As you can see, the build, measure, learn feedback loop is the process that takes leap-of-faith assumptions and tests them to see if they are valid or not. If the assumption turns out to be invalid, you pivot, finding a new leap-of-faith assumption to test for validity, and begin the build, measure, feedback loop all over again.

On the other hand, if your assumption was proven to be valid through verification of product/market fit, you are now ready to market your new product to your prospects.

FIVE

Growth

In the 30,000-foot overview we are taking to becoming an Innovative Agent, growing the business is the fourth of five steps in the process. As you well know by now, the business model presented herein is an amalgamation of other authors and thought leaders ideas, combined with a few concepts I've learned along the way in the process of building and growing My Family Health Insurance. By now, you have validated a product/market fit and are ready to move to the next step.

Innovation Accounting

After you have gone through the BML feedback loop and start to get traction with your product, you will move into the growth phase of the business model. At this stage, the entrepreneur needs to learn how to measure progress. This is done through Innovation Accounting, which refers to the process of defining, measuring and communicating progress in the business as proof that the team is learning how to grow a sustainable business.

There are two metrics Eric Ries suggests paying close attention to: Vanity Metrics and Actionable Metrics.

Vanity Metrics is data collected that is not helpful in making important decisions. Examples of vanity metrics include the number of Facebook likes you have, or the number of visits to your website or "registered users."

I call vanity metrics "happy charts." They come in all sorts of forms, bar charts, line charts, histograms, pie charts and so on. With these charts, everything looks great. They reveal real information that, seemingly, you can't ignore.

However, vanity metrics can be very deceiving. Though they may give the "all is good" signal, in reality, it couldn't be further from the truth. Below is a chart from My Family Health Insurance showing "Agent Count Since Inception." The agent count information on the Y axis shows the actual count has been deleted (so I can keep my job at My Family Health Insurance). Other than that deletion, the chart is 100% actual.

This line chart verifies that our business model is delivering what we built it for, exponential growth of recruited agents. If this was the only chart we used to measure our growth and sustainability, we could be in for a real surprise, eventually. Why? Because it leaves out very important facts that we need to know, such as:

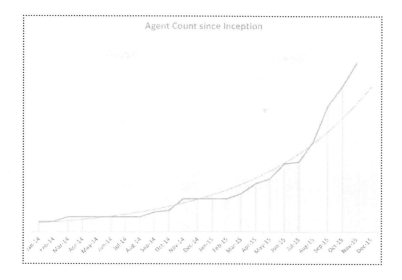

Agent Count since Inception

♀ What is the CPA, or, cost per acquisition of each recruited agent? Is it a cost that we can pay without taking on debt?

♀ What is our LTV, or, Lifetime Value of each agent recruited? Is it lower than the cost per acquisition?

♀ What about agent retention? What difference does it matter how many agents we recruit if we have a poor retention rate?

If we don't know those answers, then eventually, we could go out of business. Like a frog sitting in a pot of warm water over a burner, before we know it, we're doomed to failure.

Actionable Metrics is objective data that proves the company is truly moving towards sustainability. Examples of actionable metrics include customer acquisition costs and A/B testing.

Going back to our line chart in the previous illustration, if we knew what our CPA and LTV values were, then the line chart could be meaningful. Using My Family Health Insurance as an example, we are continuing to track our agent count because our CPA and LTV are in line.

For 2016, we continue driving our CPA down while pushing the LTV up, making the agent count a meaningful measurement. By working on all three measurements simultaneously, and other measurements as well, we are meeting our growth and sustainability targets.

The Three Engines of Growth

"The rate of growth depends primarily on three things: the profitability of each customer, the cost of acquiring a new customer and the repeat purchase rate of existing customers. The higher these values are, the faster the company will grow and the more profitable it will be. These are the drivers of the company's growth model."

— ERIC RIES

There are three engines of growth: viral, sticky and paid. Arguably, there are others, but these are the primary three. The Innovative Agent will want to use one of them (most likely the paid engine) to achieve sustainable growth. Using multiple engines of growth certainly can be done, but it is not recommended in most situations. Selecting just one engine allows you to narrow your focus, which lessens the complexity in your approach. Don't overcomplicate matters for yourself, especially, because you've made it this far! Streamline your growth engine and the results will follow.

The **viral** engine of growth takes place simply when people use your product or when people tell other people about your product. This engine is fueled either by word-of-mouth or by people experiencing your product. The viral engine of growth is very difficult to build intentionally, although it happens quite frequently.

Success or failure is based on the viral coefficient, which says that the number of referred users is equal to the total number of users. If your viral coefficient is below 1.0, any viral traffic or traction will eventually just fizzle out. For example, if you have a viral coefficient below 1.0 if every five customers bring four customers, your viral growth will eventually die out because then four friends will bring you three friends and so on to zero.

On the other hand, if your viral coefficient is more than 1.0, you will grow exponentially. If every five customers brings you six customers, which brings you seven customers, which brings you eight customers, and so on, your business model will take on a growth life all of its own!

We've experienced viral growth at My Family Health Insurance to a degree. However, the viral coefficient was below 1.0, so we've seen some viral growth spurts, but eventually they fizzled out. The agents absolutely love our value proposition and the free websites, but if each agent brings, on average, one or less agent recruits to us, the viral growth model is not sustainable.

Most businesses that use the viral growth engine trip into it by accident, which is not to say it couldn't happen for an insurance agent. Rags to riches viral growth is conceivably within anyone's reach! There are some amazing technologies out there that in the hands of the right entrepreneur could have a viral effect. Think about some of the TV commercials that have gone viral and received even more views on YouTube than the advertisers paid for primetime TV! I'm thinking specifically of the Dove ad campaign for Real Beauty (https://www.youtube.com/watch?v=XpaOjMXyJGk), some of the Old Spice ads (https://www.youtube.com/watch?v=owGykVbf-gUE) or the Gangnam Style video (https://www.youtube.com/watch?v=CH1XGdu-hzQ).

The **sticky** engine of growth is essentially an extension of the viral engine. Companies like Facebook and Twitter—that are focused almost exclusively on customer retention—use the sticky method. Their customer base is growing so quickly that they simply need to concentrate on keeping their churn rate (the annual percentage rate at which customers stop subscribing to a service) as slow as possible. The sticky engine is almost the antithesis of trying to scale your business because with this approach, companies are mostly concerned with keeping people instead of adding people.

For the purpose of this example, we'll focus on Facebook because it is the most widely used. Facebook offers free subscriptions. Just by signing up, you can be connected with anybody else in the world that is using Facebook. The company is focused on user engagement with the app. They are going to do everything possible that makes being on Facebook fun and informative, so much so that you never want to leave.

When Facebook went viral, everyone was talking about it. People around the world were saying, "Hey, you have got to check this out." All of your "friends" can keep up with your comings and goings, your news and successes, and it doesn't cost a cent. Advertisers were attracted to the steadily growing volume of eyes on the site and the more subscribers; the more they would pay to advertise. Of course, these days, we've grown accustomed to the ease of communication through this channel, but in 2004, Facebook was revolutionary.

Facebook's key focus is to continue to build the perception of value that they offer. If Facebook took away 2/3 of the features they currently offer for free, they would have a much higher attrition rate. But with a sticky model, the goal is to get existing subscribers to stay, rather than migrate away. I have a hard time seeing how Facebook's sticky engine of growth model would translate to the insurance agency, and I'm not promoting it as a model to follow, but who's to say? Anything can happen! Although most business owners dream of becoming the next Mark Zuckerburg, the likelihood of that happening is slim.

Most business owners participate in the **paid engine of growth**. The paid engine of growth requires that the value from a current customer exceeds the cost of acquiring a new customer. Marginal profit, which is the margin between your lifetime value and your cost per acquisition, determines how fast this engine of growth will be.

Compounding Profits

I'll give you another example to further clarify how the paid engine of growth works within the insurance industry. Two competing insurance agents recognize the enormous number of enrollments completed each year on the Marketplace through www.healthcare.gov. As a consumer, the Marketplace wants you to call them so you'll enroll with them. But if the agent doesn't write the business, the agent doesn't get paid. The more customers the Marketplace woos away from the local agents, the less customers there are in the pool for agents. Healthcare.gov is a major Goliath-sized competitor. The two competing insurance agents are well aware that the Marketplace is enrolling clients they would prefer to enroll. So how do they contend with the elephant in the living room?

Each of the agents built a business model, created their own MVP, completed the build-measure-learn feedback loop and validated their assumptions. Each agent used innovative accounting systems to grow a sustainable business. Both are using the paid engine of growth and employing different strategies, such as using paid Facebook ads and various other paid promotions to gain customers who might have otherwise gone through the Marketplace. Both agents did a good job of keeping the fixed costs of their business down, allowing each of them to reinvest 20% of their gains in marginal profit back into their paid engine growth models.

Both agents are seeing success and now have enough data to calculate their marginal profit. This is where the similarities end.

Agent A has a lifetime client value (LTV) of $1500.

The cost per client acquisition (CPA) is $8.

To determine your marginal profit, you simply take your lifetime value of $1500 and subtract the cost per acquisition. Agent A is making just about $1500 for each client that he or she brings on. That's very good.

Agent B has a lifetime value (LTV) of $800.

The cost per client acquisition (CPA) is $15.

Agent B is not holding onto his clients as long as Agent A and he is paying more to acquire them. Both Agents A and B are seeing great success as they grow their businesses. However, because Agent A has a marginal profit nearly double that of Agent B, the 20% that both agents are reinvesting into new advertisements is not equal. Agent A's 20% is significantly higher than Agent B's 20%. This will result in a compounding growth of business for Agent A as compared to Agent B. No doubt, both agents are experiencing compounding growth. The only difference is that Agent A's growth is compounding on a much higher scale.

As an entrepreneur, you want as wide of a spread in the margin as possible between the lifetime client value and the cost to acquire that client. Your success using the paid engine of growth depends on how wide you can make the margin.

Traditional business management books typically end the discussion on this point. Don't get me wrong; it's a vital one. In some cases, the width of the margin can be the deciding factor in the life or death of your business. However, the Innovative Agent's business model is never static and we don't ever "end." It's cyclical and always evolving and we're always looking to find a wider margin and revving up the paid engine of growth.

An Innovative Agent will continue to get better, stronger and gain more market share by:

- Continually interviewing customers to learn more about their needs.

- Always be innovating through experimentation.

- Maximizing growth by leveraging the appropriate engine of growth.

The growth of your business, and the rate of that growth, will ultimately determine the long-term health of your business. By focusing on a paid engine of growth with wide margins, your business will be well poised for long-term sustainability.

My Family Health Insurance Example

In 2015, My Family Health Insurance used the Paid Engine of Growth. Although we gladly took the low hanging fruit from the periodic and short-lived viral engine of growth, namely word of mouth, we recognized the importance of staying firmly entrenched in the Paid Engine of Growth.

We partnered with a company that has a call center that describes our product offerings to prospective agents, and then sets the appointment to speak with me. My closing ratio ran around 25% overall.

The company charged $50 per set appointment, but I had to buy 50 leads per campaign, which equated to $2,500. With a closing ratio of 25%, this meant we were acquiring roughly 13 agents per $2,500 invested.

Simple math ($2,500 / 13) showed us that our CPA (cost per acquisition) was $192 per agent. Though this was a much higher CPA than we preferred, it was an acceptable starting point since our LTV (Lifetime Value) per agent was a much higher number.

The Paid Engine of Growth worked wonders for us. For 2016, we will continue to use this engine of growth, but a $192 CPA is much too high. But not to worry, the Innovative Agent model doesn't allow for a business to remain static. Through continuous improvement, our CPAs will drop precipitously, while we continue exponential growth in agent acquisition!

Technology

Back in Chapter 1, we talked about technology being the biggest driver behind the entrepreneurial renaissance. There is a lot of fear surrounding technology, but it's not a good or bad thing; it simply is what it is (and it's not slowing down!). Technology is a little bit like a stick of dynamite. If you light the wick while you're holding it, it will blow up in your face. If your wick is a half a mile long and you light it at that distance, you can enjoy the beauty of the flames and exit before the fireworks begin. It's all about what you do with it. Technology is always getting better, faster and cheaper. In fact, it's compounding—much like Agent A's profit margin in the previous chapter.

The compounding effects have opened the door to an entrepreneurial renaissance unlike anything else we have ever seen before. The options available to entrepreneurs in today's economy are efficient, reliable and best of all, budget friendly. Practically anyone with an idea can start a business on a shoe-string budget. The roll out of new and improved technologies is moving so fast that any combination of off-the-shelf technologies could present an unlimited amount of opportunities for the Innovative Agent looking to achieve great success.

There is a widespread perception within the agent community that technology is hurting our business. Depending on how you look at technology's impact on the insurance industry, one could argue that technology has posed a threat to the old tried and true ways of doing things. Agents are losing more and more market share, but blaming technology is akin to blaming a pencil for misspelled words.

The pencil is just the instrument used by the person doing the writing. Technology is not what's hurting the agent community; it's what's behind the technology that is causing the problem.

My observations from talking with agents all across the country is that the fear of technology agents are grappling with comes primarily from two sources. The first source is simply the transition from the Industrial age to the Information age. The fundamental shift of long-held practices is being replaced with fast moving technology. The second source of fear comes from these agents watching disrupters woo their prospects away from them with technology at the core of their product offerings.

Oftentimes, fear causes people to over-react to the environment they're in, causing them to focus on fixing symptoms of a problem rather than the problem itself. In this chapter we will help you to focus more on what's behind the technology instead of on technology itself. Once you are able to objectively see that technology is not your problem, you can then focus on what you need to do to use technology to your advantage.

Getting Acquainted with Technology

As recently as 2012, at another company I am a General Agent with, we spent close to $5,000 to build a website. This website was as bare bones as it could have been. There were no bells and whistles whatsoever. Our investment into the site was several years before I learned about the low barrier to entry in the website building arena, and technology has changed dramatically since then. It's made things more accessible and cheaper across the board, in just a few short years.

At the time, I was in the same boat as a lot of other agents. It was generally accepted knowledge that if you wanted a good website, you were going to have to lay down some cash to get one. Those old notions of yesteryear are completely obsolete today. When I look back to 2012, knowing what I know now, it seems completely absurd that I would pay $5,000 for a website! Nevertheless, even today, I still encounter agents who are shelling out big bucks for websites.

Even though these agents recognize the need for a web presence, they still get caught up in the "value trap," which is a mindset that says, "If I'm going to get a lot of value out of my website, I should probably pay a lot of money for it." This mindset could not be further from the truth today.

The Ah-Ha Moment

In 2014, at My Family Health Insurance we recognized that we had to take advantage of fast-moving technology, not only because it made sense, but also because technology was going to help us shift the paradigm of how we competed in the insurance industry. It was a very difficult transition, but we knew we were doing what was needed, reinforced by leaders in lean thinking, such as Ries, Maurya and Christensen.

Once we understood the need for technology, we also knew it was time to get some help. We called on a local website designer and overall technology guru named Tim. Together, we talked about our vision of providing our agent partners value that no other GA was offering. We weren't entirely sure what it would be.

Through much discussion, Tim moved us in the direction of offering prospects free landing pages and eventually a free website. He knew we were low on resources, unfamiliar with website development and on a tight budget. But, he pushed forward, and described the benefits our agents would get with our offerings, to which we fully agreed.

At this point, we became convinced that landing pages and eventually a website would be our MVP. The question then moved to costs and logistics. Tim's hourly fee was steep for our budget. How could we pay him to develop websites with limited resources? The other question was how could Tim find the time to develop websites for recruited agents while he was working in a full-time career?

The next and obvious question was, "Is it possible for us to build landing pages and websites on our tight budget and without internal expertise in website development?" He just grinned and said, "Of course!" He went on to explain to us how simple and affordable it was to build websites in this day and age. We were shocked and elated to learn that what we had been hoping for was not only a possibility, but also a realistic goal! It was a huge ah-ha moment for us.

Our excitement led to a deeper discussion about technology and the opportunities we could capture with it. We started to think about things in a completely new way. Tim had enlightened us and there was no turning back!

In order to compete in today's market place, Innovative Agents need to have their own ah-ha moments with technology. If, like most people, you are baffled and terrified by how it all works, do what we did and talk to a professional! Some agents have already embraced technology, but a lot of agents are still holding onto a lot of fear. If you fall into the latter category, a consultative meeting with the right person will make all the difference.

It's worth mentioning, I do not have a background in a field of technology. Just the opposite. In the office, I am often heckled because, although I see the big picture of how technology should work in a business, I am much slower at grasping the details and various applications than the rest of the team. It's kind of like a toddler that goes from crawling, to walking and then eventually learning how to run. And actually, I'm fine with it. Because with practice comes habit.

Finding "Your Ryan"

You are an entrepreneur, not an engineer. This means there is no need whatsoever for you to get caught up in the logistics or mechanics of how technology works. It is sufficient for you to simply embrace the concept behind the various technologies available to you and envision how they may be a fit for your business or product. Understanding this was a challenge that I faced because I have always been the type of person who wants to know the why behind everything. When it comes to technology and how it actually works, it was hard for me to accept that I was not the best person to push all of the buttons or turn all of the knobs. There are people with far more knowledge and advanced skills to fiddle around with the technicalities of technology. As the entrepreneur, it can be very difficult being the engineer too.

You're the big idea person on your team. Heck, you may even be the only person on your team, which is even more of a reason to outsource the areas that you cannot contribute to your highest abilities. Trying to do it all will only bog you down and drain you of your time and energy. So, stick to what you do best and focus on the big picture outcome.

For the independent agents at home or in the smaller shops, because of limited resources, consider outsourcing or hiring an employee to handle the nuts and bolts of the technology piece. I say this because small businesses don't have the luxury of taking much time away from selling. Early on, My Family Health Insurance was in this position. As much as we didn't want to admit it, we just couldn't afford to outsource all of our technology needs to our guru, Tim. Little did we know, Tim's replacement was sitting right under our nose.

In the months leading up to this point, and for the purposes of filling a sales position in our organization, we hired Ryan, a 26-year-old millennial (who grew up with technology). He was new to insurance sales, but he was gradually getting better. Whenever we had team meetings that didn't involve him, Ryan almost always found a way of becoming a part of the meeting anyway. His curiosity about the growth of the agency got the best of him. Truth be told, he couldn't have shown up at a better time, just as we were exploring various technologies and processes.

Ryan's input blew us away. He schooled us on many different technologies and how they can be applied to business situations. Before long, it seemed Ryan was introducing new concepts and technologies almost by the week. No matter what task we were up against, Ryan just took it in stride, without fear and without hesitation.

Ryan now guides "everything technological" in our operations. Needless to say, he comes at a lower cost than having to outsource. Before spending a lot of money outsourcing, look at your local pool of millennials. If you can find someone like ours, technology will be the least of your worries.

Using Technology to Build Your Strategy

My Family Health Insurance was determined to choose one or more free (or very low cost) off-the-shelf technologies as part of our product. That's how we were able to offer a free website to onboarding agents.

Just as we were innovative in finding technologies for our product, we were also innovative in creating our strategy—the process that delivers our product (free website) to our agent partners. We focused on every aspect, from agent recruitment, to processing new agent contact information to website development.

The technologies we found for our strategy were truly amazing. They were simple to use, easy to implement, and just as importantly, they were free or very inexpensive. These technologies helped us to streamline our internal processes, making us extraordinarily more efficient than we were prior to acquiring them.

I'll share a few examples of the problems we had to tackle and which free (or very low-cost) technologies we used to resolve them.

Problem #1: We needed a way to collect, update and publish important information between team members who were not all located in the same office.

We needed to have access to a common folder so that no matter where anyone was or what device they were using, everyone on the team could locate the information they needed.

Solution: Dropbox

Cost: FREE

Problem #2: We needed a screen-sharing program so I could present our offering effectively to current and prospective agents. This problem was actually two fold, in that the key to onboarding new agents is to strike while the iron is hot. We wanted to be able to get in front of the agents at the precise moment they expressed interest in learning more about our product. Hot leads sell better than cold leads.

Also, most people are visual learners. We knew if we could find a technology that allowed us to pick up the phone, call a hot lead and say, "Do you have a few minutes so I can walk you through our product?"—we were that much closer to bringing them on board. Screen sharing would allow us the opportunity to share all of the bells and whistles with the same level of interaction as if we were sitting right in front of our prospects in an office. And the best part? It doesn't cost a penny!

Solution: Join.me

Cost: FREE

Problem #3: Coordinating meetings with prospective agents can be very time consuming. Emailing to find a time that works for both parties can sometimes take up to a few days of back and forth. People across industries have experienced this problem, which can be a real bottleneck in business. Whether you work in sales or you're trying to coordinate a church event, a fundraiser, or even a get together with friends or family, email scheduling can be a nightmare.

Rather than continuing to fight the scheduling battle, we found a solution to streamline the process. Our bread and butter is in high volume connections to prospective agents through the marketing agencies we work with. We need to be able to communicate with them effectively and efficiently to demonstrate our offering so they can make a decision. If scheduling roadblocks bog us down, our productivity takes a nosedive.

With a simple technology tool, prospective agents can pick an open spot on my calendar that suits their schedule. I have control over the times and dates that I am available, and I'm sent an alert when a new appointment has been scheduled. All of this while protecting the privacy of the appointments I already have. This tool has drastically reduced appointment scheduling activities. Today, I couldn't live without it. It sounds like the perfect MVP doesn't it?

Solution: Calendly

Cost: $8/month

Problem #4: We needed forms for many purposes such as websites, surveys, campaigns, agent information and more. These fillable forms have become absolutely invaluable to us for market testing new ideas and soliciting customer feedback on existing products. They allow us to keep our forms fresh and timely, plus they offer another valuable touch point with our prospects and clients.

Solution: EmailMeForm

Cost: $9.95/month

My Family Health Insurance had far more than four problems to contend with! I wanted to give a sample of some common issues that most small business owners face and provide some easy and cost effective solutions that work across industries. The total monthly cost for these four critical technological solutions is a whopping $17.95 per month. I can't begin to put a price on the value they have given us.

A Missed Opportunity

As you know, My Family Health Insurance recruits agents into our down line through our value added proposition. The more agents we bring in, the more profitable we are. This business strategy is straightforward, but there is a dual side to our strategy as well. If we can present technologies to an agent that helps them sell, communicate and connect with their prospects better, they will increase their sales, thus helping us to increase our profits as well. As previously mentioned, in our attempts to help the down line agents sell more products more efficiently, we offer various electronic direct enrollment portals (EDEP's). These portals are simply electronic tools to enroll people in a product such as dental, vision, medical, or health insurance.

My Family Health Insurance offers one EDEP that provides agent partners the opportunity to dramatically increase their income during the Open Enrollment Period (Marketplace enrollments only). It is not a free portal, but the small cost of this EDEP absolutely dwarfs the income potential it offers agent partners that understands the incredible leverage it delivers as compared to the free EDEPS provided by insurance companies and other competitors.

The INXSCloud Broker Program (www.my1hr.com) has one element that is singularly unique, which is an enrollment data form. The form is sent to prospects to complete via e-mail. When they return the form, it migrates into a quoting tool, which allows the agent to quickly quote options and pricing. It also makes adjustments for subsidy and cost-share.

The agent can create up to four options and e-mail it back to the prospect. Next, the agent picks up the phone and reviews those options with the prospect. In the end, a plan is chosen and the agent then proceeds to enroll the prospect through the broker channel at healthcare.gov. It's just that simple.

There are several other similar portals such available for agents to choose. However, no other portal is set up to send and retrieve enrollment data forms in this manner. You may be asking, what's the difference? A lot! Based on a very large sample of prospects that completed and returned the enrollment data form, **over 97%** converted from prospect to client!

Our findings have nothing whatsoever to do with the portal. The reason why agents are seeing over a 97% conversion rate is because of the process of connecting easily and conveniently with their prospects. Agents do not have to "touch" the prospects any more than is absolutely necessary. For the prospect, the entire transaction is completed within three easy steps:

1. Complete the enrollment form and return it to the agent.

2. Review options with agent.

3. Agent enrolls the prospect in a plan that is right for him or her.

Astonishingly, less than 30% of our agents are using the INXS Cloud direct enrollment portal, despite the staggering 97+% prospect conversion rate.

Agent partners that don't use this portal say they are not attracted to the portal because:

1. It's too expensive. The portal they are currently using is free.

2. There's not enough difference between the portals to make the switch.

3. They are comfortable working with the portal they are already using.

Choosing not to purchase the INXS Cloud portal was based on the agent's perceived value of one portal as compared to another. Instead of looking at the INXS Cloud portal as a potential to better connect with prospects (resulting in substantially higher sales and less time per enrollment), they instead chose to focus on the portal, a classic example of not understanding the value they would get by giving a customer what they're looking for.

When agents apply the Innovative Agent principles, disconnections like this is less frequent. Instead of comparing one EDEP with another EDEP, the agent will instead ask, "which of these two EDEP's better connects me with my prospects?"

The Innovative Agent sees challenges differently than the average agent. I've written this book to serve as your roadmap, a simple five-step process that boils down some of the strategies and concepts I've used and implemented with much success at My Family Health Insurance. This is not meant to be a comprehensive, how-to guide, but rather a 30,000-foot view of the insurance landscape and an overview of a one-of-a-kind roadmap to survive and thrive in insurance sales. The advice herein is coming from somebody who's been in the trenches, who's felt these same fears and who's experienced the same feeling of overwhelm. I've had to be resourceful, dig deep and adopt an innovative mindset in order to succeed.

The worries of the typical agent, as outlined in Chapter One, are now recognized as a much bigger problem. We have been lacking a suitable business model sufficient to meet the challenges we face today, until now. Instead of seeing disruptive innovators as a serious threat to your business, you are equipped to disrupt markets and grow your business yourself using the five Innovative Agent principles shared in this book.

By now, your focus has likely shifted to the most important part of your business—your customers. It's not just about connecting with them; it's about understanding what they really want and retaining them for a lifetime. Through constant experimentation, you are able to provide them with the product and service that fits their unique lifestyle and needs. You now know how to meet them on their terms.

Failure is now seen through a different lens than it was before. An Innovative Agent knows that failure, though painful, is the best way to learn about your customers. You know that when you face a failure, the biggest takeaway is that you better know your prospect. And, you can select a new MVP that is more in alignment with the customers' needs while still adhering to the vision of your company. You will return time and time again to the Build-Measure-Learn feedback loop for continuous improvement.

You're innovating through experimentation, giving you a dual effect—to connect with your customers, while also streamlining your internal processes. You're setting yourself apart from your competitors by giving consumers a much better reason to do business with you. Innovation is your backbone.

Most importantly, you have peace of mind. You're now in firm control of your business with a very clear understanding of how to run it.

Your income opportunities during this entrepreneurial renaissance are almost limitless because you have the mind of the entrepreneur and you have the roadmap to get the job done. You can reach for whatever you want to take in the market, whether you want to disrupt across the United States or focus on a smaller market. It's your call. It's your business. It's your dream. Re-energize your passion by doing what you do best—selling insurance!

To continue your journey, please visit:

www.theinnovativeagent.com

N O T E S

1. https://en.wikipedia.org/wiki/Disruptive_innovation

2. http://www.pewinternet.org/2013/01/31/in-store-mobile-commerce-during-the-2012-holiday-shopping-season/

3. http://thisweekinstartups.com/mark-cuban-kick-ass/

4. https://en.wikipedia.org/wiki/Groupthink

5. https://en.wikipedia.org/wiki/Zenefits

6. https://en.wikipedia.org/wiki/Product/market_fit

The Author

MARK SISSON specializes in providing insurance agents education, innovative programs and concepts to meet the challenges of fast moving technology and disruption that's so prevalent in the insurance industry today.

Having worked for more than 17 years in the insurance industry, Mark has recently expanded his services to the insurance industry as instructor and author.

Mark continues to progress his passion of providing the tools and education insurance agents need so they can most effectively compete in this technology-driven environment.

Made in the USA
Lexington, KY
27 March 2016